BIRDS OF WISCONSIN

Publication of this book is sponsored by

FRIENDS OF THE MUSEUM, INC.

American Woodcock
See page 212

BIRDS
OF
WISCONSIN

OWEN J. GROMME

Assisted by WARREN P. DETTMANN

and by the staff of the Milwaukee Public Museum

Published for

The Milwaukee Public Museum by

The University of Wisconsin Press

MADISON, 1964

Published by
THE UNIVERSITY OF WISCONSIN PRESS
Mailing address: P.O. Box 1379, Madison, Wisconsin 53701
Editorial offices: 430 Sterling Court, Madison

Copyright © 1963 by the Friends of the Museum, Inc.
Second printing, 1964

Manufactured in the United States of America
Engravings by Mueller Engraving Company, Milwaukee, Wisconsin
Composition and printing by Moebius Printing Company, Milwaukee, Wisconsin
Binding by the Boehm Bindery Company, Milwaukee, Wisconsin

Jacket engraved by Mueller Engraving Company, printed by Moebius Printing Company
Map of Wisconsin drafted by the University of Wisconsin Cartographic Laboratory

Library of Congress Catalog Card Number 63-15055

Foreword

The Milwaukee Public Museum has been a continuing source of pride to residents of this city since its founding in 1883. This book is both the climax of one of the most ambitious and extended of the museum's programs and a tribute to the interest which this organization has aroused and sustained in the community. *Birds of Wisconsin* has been a long time in the making and is the result of the co-operative efforts of many individuals and civic groups. One of these groups, Friends of the Museum, Incorporated, was formed in the fall of 1959. The articles of incorporation and bylaws dedicated its efforts toward charitable, scientific, and educational activities especially designed to foster and promote the Milwaukee Public Museum. The Friends selected as their first major project the publication of this book, which had already had so much effort and artistry expended in its behalf.

It is a pleasure for me to write about my friend, Owen J. Gromme, the curator of the museum's Division of Birds and Mammals. Mr. Gromme began painting this series of portraits of birds known to be native to this north central habitat in 1941, when he was already recognized nationally as one of the outstanding wildlife artists of our time. His watercolor sketch of three Shoveler Ducks in flight was used on the 1945-46 Migratory Bird Hunting stamp. Completion of these paintings took him over twenty years, since he could work only part time on the project. As Curator of Birds and Mammals, Mr. Gromme has headed a competent staff of ornithologists who have carefully assembled the scientific data on which *Birds of Wisconsin* is based. As a result, this publication is more than just a superb collection of paintings of Wisconsin birds; it is also a valuable guide to the range, nesting areas, and migration habits of these 328 species.

How fortunate Wisconsin was on that day in the early 1920's, when Owen Gromme was visited in his museum office by the great Louis Agassiz Fuertes, who asked him to come to Ithaca, New York, as an understudy. Mr. Gromme decided to stay in Wisconsin where soon we, like Fuertes, recognized in Gromme's work a sensitive talent to recreate a living-likeness in a natural habitat.

This sympathetic awareness of the living soul and its integral relation to the ecological whole was understood and recognized by Fuertes and is in strong evidence in the works of both men. This basic sense of the natural and love for the living, derived from boyhoods spent freely observing natural history in the country, was experienced by both artists, and developed a credo of integrity of truth that may best be described in a letter of Fuertes' to one of his many pupils in which he stated in part:

. . . for God's sake be honest, and strive for what seems to you true and lovely. I should say that more high aspiration has been egoized into mediocrity than has withstood the terrible ordeal of passing through a human soul for its interpretation. . . . I still stick out for knowledge—good, sound, deep, and appreciative knowledge—as the one fundamental basic pre-requisite of all art, and particularly of naturalistic art. . . . Great lovers have all had their admiring audience; great lovers of natural truth perhaps less than others. But that is my simple credo: it's easy, however, to "believe" in truth, as an abstract conception; quite another thing to discover and crystallize this truth into visible and permanent form. That's a hard job, and most artists would rather pass the buck, and in place of hard-wrought unadorned truth, present the gog-eyed world with the decorative by-products of their efforts, not so much for truth as for originality. . . . [*Louis Agassiz Fuertes,* edited by Mary Fuertes Boynton, N.Y.: Oxford Univ. Press, 1956, pp. 239–40.]

To me this best describes the art of Owen J. Gromme, not mere self-expression but a manifestation of truth.

The plates of *Birds of Wisconsin* are indicative of this philosophy, and are divided into two categories for your enjoyment. The first segment consists of formal plates for identification following the normal nomenclature as prescribed in the A.O.U. Check-list; with a second gallery composed of informal paintings, creating an ecological relationship of subject to its natural environment. Scenes throughout our state are recaptured. Each revives a pleasant moment in the memory of the individual reader.

The scope of the book historically embraces much of the past and present in the ever-constant changing of our bird community. The Passenger Pigeon (Plate 40), last recorded in Wisconsin in 1899, is certainly a tragic portrait of the lack of man's understanding of his relationship to other living things. The Brewer's Blackbird (Plate 77), first seen in the state within the last twenty years, and the most recent newcomer, the Cattle Egret (Plate 89), render stark testimony to this constant change. This is again in evidence with the western penetration of the Western Meadowlark (Plate 74) and the southern ingress of the spectacular Cardinal (Plate 80). The Wild Turkey (Plate 24), having disappeared completely from the state, has been successfully re-introduced, and with proper management could be maintained.

While some species struggle for their survival, like the Greater Prairie Chicken (Plate 22), others like the Pileated Woodpecker (Plate 48), have adapted themselves to their changing community and have slowly increased their numbers. The magnificent Sandhill Cranes (page 199), painted in an airy exhibit of buoyancy and balanced beauty, are also displaying a recent comeback. They probably represent our oldest form of bird life as it is known in the state. Their ancestors, with lineage in the Eocene epoch some forty million years ago, stridently trumpeted their sonorous sky song high above the glacier-gripped land.

The publication's flowing continuity of one man's art is rare among published bird books today. The consistent richness of the backgrounds produces an over-all completeness and is a credit to the artist's understanding of his subject and his feeling toward color and form.

The inclusion of the informal plates gives the reader the opportunity to see some of our native species painted in the fullness of their habitat by a great and versatile artist. The decision to include these plates created additional challenges, not only because of the increased cost of reproducing the paintings, but other complications. As none of these informal plates was painted for reproduction—most were in the hands of private collectors and some were the private property of the author himself—they had to be assembled. They are reproduced in this book through the courtesy of the owners, for which we are deeply indebted. Our thanks to: Hermann A. Nunnemacher, Arthur Mac-Arthur, Harold P. Mueller, Sr., Roy O. Gromme, Dr. Alfred Wallner, Mr. and Mrs. Frank C. Howard, Jr., Dr. William Taylor, and Mrs. Parker Poe.

Friends of the Museum, Incorporated, is indebted to many who have made the publication possible. A deluxe edition of two hundred copies of the book was sold at $100 per copy, and to each of these purchasers we extend our thanks. Especially notable within this group are the Jos. Schlitz Brewing Company and the Robert A. Uihlein family.

The additional financing for publication of the informal plates was made possible by special gifts from the Charles W. Wright Foundation of Badger Meter, Inc., the Milwaukee Journal, First Wisconsin Foundation, Inc., M. U. and A. C. Elser Foundation, Rahr Foundation, Guido R. Rahr Foundation, Trepte Family Fund, Mr. Willis G. Sullivan, Mr. and Mrs. Herbert P. Brumder, Blackhawk Foundation, Mr. and Mrs. Walter G. Zinn, Galland-Henning Manufacturing Co., Vogel Foundation, Inc., Marshall and Ilsley Bank, and Mr. and Mrs. Arthur MacArthur. Special contributions included one in memory of Walter Sherman Ott, and a gift in co-operation with the Society of *Tympanuchus Cupido Pinnatus*, Ltd.

The Mueller Engraving Company has long demonstrated its faith in this publication, and it is no exaggeration to state that without this steadfast faith the book could not have been published. Years before publication was a certainty, they had demonstrated this faith by capturing the perishable colors on copper plates. Mr. Richard A. Shilbauer and Mr. Julius Mueller have our sincere and cordial thanks.

The Moebius Printing Company has co-operated very closely with the Friends, and has contributed a great deal toward successful publication. They have accomplished with great skill and fidelity their part in the printing of an outstanding book in the field of graphic ornithology.

This foreword would not be complete without special mention of the skillful work of Thomas Ehrlich, who served as special legal counsel in making the many and complicated arrangements whereby this publication became a reality. I also wish to thank C. P. Fox who originally suggested that the inclusion of the sixteen informal plates would greatly enhance the value and popular appeal of the book, because the activities of birds in their natural environment could not be shown adequately in the formal plates.

Finally, I wish to express my appreciation to Arthur J. Frank, J. William Stack, Jr., George M. Chester, and John F. Dahlberg for their invaluable suggestions and direction, and to all the Friends of the Museum for their support of this publication which will enhance the story of Wisconsin's natural environment and resources, provide a purposeful educational benefit to those who now enjoy our avian wildlife, and awaken in those yet to come the enduring interest and love of the beauty of the outdoor world.

FREDERICK L. OTT
President, Friends of the Museum, Inc.

Acknowledgments

Publication of an up-to-date book on the birds of Wisconsin was long considered by the Milwaukee Public Museum, but serious planning was deferred because of the financial problems inherent in colored reproduction. Private subscription seemed to be the only possible means to raise the necessary funds and the museum was reluctant to expend the effort required to solicit so large an amount of money. In 1941 Mr. George Weinhagen, Jr., suggested that some of my paintings of Wisconsin birds be reproduced in book form and backed his faith by a gift of $400 to be deposited in what later became known as the "Birds of Wisconsin Trust Fund." With this initial encouragement and with the enthusiastic approval of Dr. Ira Edwards, who was then director of the museum, the necessary legal arrangements were made and the museum board of trustees approved a publication project based upon subscription to a patrons' edition of the book. Following Mr. Weinhagen's lead, many civic-minded citizens and firms contributed to the fund.

But completion of the paintings and compilation of accompanying textual materials progressed much more rapidly than funds accumulated. The problem of continuing the work came to the attention of Mr. Robert A. Uihlein, Sr., vice-president of the Jos. Schlitz Brewing Company, who enhanced the fund by a gift of several thousand dollars in the name of his firm. Meanwhile, the Mueller Engraving Company of Milwaukee, which had been selected to do the color-process work, went ahead at their own risk and produced a large portion of the color engravings so that proofs could be used to assist in raising funds.

We were still far from our financial goal when Mr. Frederick L. Ott of Milwaukee enlisted the support of other young Milwaukee business executives in forming Friends of the Museum, Incorporated, whose initial project was to complete the publication trust fund. Through his untiring and persistent efforts our financial goal was finally attained.

A variety of duties connected with compilation of data and preparation of artwork were shared by many members of the museum staff and volunteer workers. Particular commendation is due Mr. Warren Dettmann and Mr. John L. Diedrich of the museum staff. Mr. Dettmann devoted many painstaking hours to delineation of the silhouettes and execution of the artwork for the identification pages facing the 89 formal portraits, and Mr. Diedrich indexed thousands of pages of my personal field notes and rendered other valuable assistance in preparing material for use on maps and date lines. Both also assisted me greatly in checking the color proofs. Mr. Harvey J. Mayer, also of the museum staff, contributed particularly to preparation of statistical material. For volunteer service at the museum, Mr. Clarence S. Jung and Mr. H. W. Schaars deserve special thanks. Many others contributed their efforts to the collection and organization of data to be used in a volume of text which will eventually be published as a technical supplement to this volume of plates. The author looks forward to the opportunity of thanking more of these individuals by name in the second publication.

To the many who contributed financial aid and extraordinary personal effort the Milwaukee Public Museum and particularly the author owe a debt of sincere gratitude.

OWEN J. GROMME

March, 1963

Contents

Introduction

Since publication of *The Birds of Wisconsin* by L. Kumlien and N. Hollister in 1903, the increase and shift in human population and the consequent expansion of agriculture and increased use of natural resources have drastically altered the face of our land. In the last several decades the change in wildlife environment has been particularly accelerated, with marked effects on bird populations. In the areas affected, the changed conditions have often given rise to the reappearance of long-absent forms or the disappearance of whole species.

Modern transportation, more leisure time, easier access to remote areas, and newly developed mechanical aids for study have created a rapidly growing interest in birds. Some observers are interested in ecological relationships of birds insofar as they affect other living things or our everyday lives and well-being; others love birds for their beauty of form and song; and nearly all of us are fascinated by them just because they are birds.

To satisfy the desire for greater ornithological knowledge, the Milwaukee Public Museum has long wished to publish an up-to-date book on the birds of Wisconsin. The original publication plan gradually formulated through the years called for a detailed text accompanied by color plates in a single volume, but this was altered when work on the color section was completed first. The present publication of the plates only was the result of a desire to make the identification portraits available for public use without further delay. Work on an accompanying text continues in expectation of a second volume to complete the original plan.

The similarity of Wisconsin's topography and climate to that of neighboring states in the Great Lakes area will make this book of portraits useful well beyond state boundaries. All species of birds recorded here are known to visit, pass through, or reside in the state for all or part of the year. The plates are arranged to conform as nearly as possible with the fifth (1957) edition of *Check-list of North American Birds* prepared by the American Ornithologists' Union, but many engravings were completed while revisions of the fourth (1931) edition were in progress. In conformity with procedures followed in the arrangement of the new list in which the effort to provide vernacular names for subspecies was abandoned, we have placed the emphasis on the species. In the few cases where subspecies were featured on plates completed before A.O.U. revisions, the vernacular names are shown in parentheses to lessen confusion, and a "see" reference is made to the illustration of the form bearing the general common name, as on Plate 6 in the case of

(Richardson's) Canada Goose. Synonyms and older vernacular names used earlier by the A.O.U. will be found in the index. Classifiers' names, which normally follow the names of species, were omitted in the identification legends facing the plates because of typographical complications, but they are contained in the index following entries of scientific names.

It was difficult to determine which birds not to illustrate. With the exception of Barrow's Goldeneye, birds technically classified as being "hypothetical" were excluded, the classification indicating that reliable sight records for these species do occur but that these records are not substantiated by identifiable photographs or by specimens. Plate 11, where Barrow's Goldeneye is depicted and described as accidental, was executed before it was discovered that an erroneous record invalidated the accepted status of this species.

Hypothetical species not illustrated

Ammodramus bairdii, Baird's Sparrow
Chen rossii, Ross' Goose
Contopus sordidulus, Western Wood Pewee
Cygnus olor, Mute Swan
Dendroica auduboni, Audubon's Warbler
Dendroica kirtlandii, Kirtland's Warbler
Falco mexicanus, Prairie Falcon
Hydranassa tricolor, Louisiana Heron
Lagopus lagopus, Willow Ptarmigan
Larus atricilla, Laughing Gull
Larus glaucoides, Iceland Gull
Larus minutus, Little Gull
Oenanthe oenanthe, Wheatear
Passerina amoena, Lazuli Bunting
Passerina ciris, Painted Bunting
Philomachus pugnax, Ruff
Plegadis chihi, white-faced Ibis
Pyrocephalus rubinus, Vermilion Flycatcher
Sterna dougallii, Roseate Tern

Some species long extinct in the state, such as the Carolina Parakeet, are not shown. The Passenger Pigeon, however, is featured because it was so spectacular in point of numbers, figured so prominently in early state history, and is such an outstanding object lesson in what can result when a resource is ruthlessly exploited. Other accidental birds were reluctantly excluded for reasons of economy.

Accidental and extinct species not illustrated

Ajaia ajaja, Roseate Spoonbill
Amphispiza bilineata, Black-throated Sparrow
Anas bahamensis, Bahama Duck
Carduelis carduelis, European Goldfinch

Charadrius alexandrinus, Snowy Plover
Chlidonias leucopterus, White-winged Black Tern
Chlorura chlorura, Green-tailed Towhee
Conuropsis carolinensis, Carolina Parakeet (extinct)
Fregata magnificens, Magnificent Frigate-bird
Himantopus mexicanus, Black-necked Stilt
Icterus bullockii, Bullocks's Oriole
Ixoreus naevius, Varied Thrush
Muscivora forficata, Scissor-tailed Flycatcher
Nucifraga columbiana, Clark's Nutcracker
Olor buccinator, Trumpeter Swan (formerly not
    uncommon)
Oxyura dominica, Masked Duck
Pagophila eburnea, Ivory Gull
Plautus alle, Dovekie
Rissa tridactyla, Black-legged Kittiwake
Sayornis saya, Say's Phoebe
Sialia currucoides, Mountain Bluebird
Somateria mollissima, Common Eider
Stercorarius longicaudus, Long-tailed Jaeger
Synthliboramphus antiquum, Ancient Murrelet
Xema sabini, Sabine's Gull

For quick reference, the visual aid of an accurate illustration in color is often worth a page of written description. Serious consideration was given the various means by which color plates could be presented within the limitation of available funds. A page for each species would have been ideal but at the same time very costly. In the plan finally selected we believe that the over-all advantage of showing more birds in color outweighs the resulting disadvantage of an occasional crowded plate.

The subjects are presented as they would be seen under ordinary field conditions in the open and in average light, rather than in the laboratory. Shadows are used in a manner so as not to submerge identifying ground color insofar as possible. In most instances, with due allowance for space limitation, the birds are shown in the environment in which they can be found in Wisconsin and neighboring states.

Where space or color combination permits, the species within the genera are shown together on a page, but on several plates birds of different genera are shown because of size difficulties or for comparison. The Great Blue Heron and cranes share the same plate because the term "crane" is generally used with reference to either.

On most plates each bird is shown in proportion to the others without regard for perspective. When birds of extreme variance in size are shown on the same plate, the larger birds are represented in the background in perspective proportion. The fractional size of the subjects is noted below the title of the plate. Those portions of birds of either sex that are concealed from view by foliage or for other reasons of composition may be assumed to be similar to the other sex which is fully shown. Where possible, without too much distortion, the bird is shown in a position that will best reveal its identifying field marks or flash colors, while at the same time the normal position has been kept in mind.

On some plates the nests, eggs, or young have been included, and it is hoped that the addition of this identification, so often slighted in ornithological portraits, will add interest and value to the work. In several instances the general type of nest illustrated closely resembles that of other species of the same genus not shown on the plate. In others, nests are included as a means of distinguishing between adults of species similar in appearance. The Acadian Flycatcher, for example, which so closely resembles Traill's Flycatcher, is shown at its nest because the difference in nest types is one certain means of distinguishing between the two species in the field. The male hummingbird, which is known to keep away from the nest, appears on a plate containing a nest; and the sphinx moth, which is so often mistaken for a hummingbird, is represented on the same plate for comparison.

The inclusion of several subjects on a plate represented environmental as well as seasonal difficulties to the artist, especially where birds appear both in summer and winter plumages, but due allowance for this must be made by the reader. On several of the plates where some birds are shown in flight and others are at rest, it should be understood that the general flight contours are characteristic of the genus.

While it was seldom possible to illustrate birds' ecological relationships to each other within a plate, the ecological relationship of a bird to its environment was respected within the limitations of background composition. Such preferences of habitat as boggy ground or particular types of vegetation for nesting or roosting were illustrated insofar as groupings of species permitted.

The turkey plate was done in oil. All of the other 88 portraits in the first section of the book were done in water color. The painting for the hummingbird plate, the first to be done, was completed in 1942, and it was also the subject for the first engraving. The last two paintings, now Plates 24 and 89, were completed in 1962. Plate 89 shows species recently added to the state list and others which, for various reasons, were not included in the normal order of species.

The foregoing explanation of artistic restrictions applies to the 89 numbered plates which constitute the first portion of this book. The sixteen additional plates of birds in action and in habitat, which are reproduced as the frontispiece and on pages 183 through 211, were not painted with reproduction in mind and are not intended as formal identification portraits. They represent the author's attempts to share with the reader a few of the actual events or observations of many years of field work. Minor liberties were taken in cropping the originals to scale the engravings to a uniform size, but in these plates there were no restraining elements of composition or crowding and a truer illustration of ecological relationships between birds and animals and of typical habitats was possible.

Data consulted in compiling the information on distribution and nesting which faces the formal portraits were derived from a variety of unpublished and published sources. Chief among the unpublished materials were the records of the Milwaukee Public Museum, the field notes of the author, and charts submitted by many co-operators from various parts of the state. The principal journals consulted were *The Passenger Pigeon, Audubon Magazine, Auk, Wilson Bulletin,* and *The Wisconsin Conservation Bulletin.* The major books were *The Birds of Wisconsin* (1951) by L. Kumlien and N. Hollister with revisions by A. W. Schorger, and *A Half Century of Change in Bird Populations of the Lower Chippewa River, Wisconsin* by Irvin O. Buss and Helmer Mattison. Particularly valuable was the booklet, *Wisconsin Birds: A Checklist with Migration Charts* by N. R. Barger, Roy H. Lound, and Samuel D. Robbins, Jr., with a bibliography by A. W. Schorger, which was published by the Wisconsin Society for Ornithology in 1960. From the example of this publication we devised a similar system of date lines and adopted the terms to describe status.

The notations accompanying the formal portraits are designed to show at a glance the name of the bird, where and when it can be found within Wisconsin, and if and when it nests in the state. Sex of the bird illustrated is indicated near the silhouette by the standard symbols for male ♂ and for female ♀ . When sexes are alike in color pattern, only one bird is shown and it bears the symbol of both male and female. Unless otherwise indicated, all birds shown are adults in breeding plumage.

Date lines

The chart accompanying all except occasional rare or accidental species is divided into twelve segments lettered for the months of the year. The period of normal occurrence of the species in Wisconsin is indicated by a solid line drawn through the lower part of this date line. Periods of build-up or tapering off during migration or isolated dates are indicated by a broken line. A shorter line occurring on the upper part of this date line indicates the nesting period for those species which breed in the state. The time indicated is the average time from the laying of the first egg until the young leave the nest and includes the time difference for those species which produce a second or third brood of young. In general, the time of greatest nesting activity is during the first part of the period indicated, since many species raise but one brood a year. Both the periods of occurrence and nesting are slightly generalized to represent an average for the state as a whole and due allowance should be made for variations in the extreme northern and southern parts of the state.

Maps

The small maps accompanying most species are variously colored yellow, blue, or green, indicating occurrence in the summer, in the winter, or through the year, respectively. In so small a map, areas of occurrence had to be highly generalized and technical problems precluded the use of graduated shades to indicate degrees of population density. Solid color, therefore, implies general range but does not always include isolated areas where a species has been or could be found. In some cases color was extended to include probable areas occurring between sites of known occurrence.

The use of color on the maps was influenced by the currency of sight records for any given area, with the intention that an observer interested in sighting a particular species would be directed to a particular area of the state. Former range as described by earlier writers was not indicated. A stylized arrow is sometimes used on an uncolored map to indicate that a species migrates through Wisconsin but does not reside in the state. It is also used to indicate transients or winter visitants in scattered parts of the state other than those residence areas indicated by color, particularly when it was appropriate to use color on relatively small or scattered areas of the map.

Descriptive terms

A further refinement of distribution is indicated by use of the word "local" or "locally" in the description of the status of the bird. This indicates occurrences of particular species in restricted areas of preference which may be more or less widely separated. Thus, on Plate 75 the Yellow-headed Blackbird, which occurs in isolated colonies at Horicon Marsh and a few other swamps, is described as a "fairly common summer resident locally."

Some species of waterfowl occur throughout the winter in localized ice-free places below dams or in open spots on the larger inland lakes or Lake Michigan, often at widely separated points. The distribution of these points of winter residence for various species accounts for the variations in patterns of color on the maps, with solid blue for the entire state being used to indicate areas of occurrence so evenly distributed as those where the Common Merganser is found.

The status descriptions defined below are adapted with slight modifications from the previously mentioned checklist published by the Wisconsin Society for Ornithology.

Permanent resident: present at all seasons.

Summer resident: present throughout summer, but not necessarily as a breeder.

Winter resident: present throughout winter.

Transient visitant: present during migration period or as a wanderer.

Summer visitant: present during part or parts of summer.

Winter visitant: present during part or parts of winter.

Abundant: conspicuously numerous.

Common: noticeably numerous but less than abundant.

Fairly common, uncommon, rare, and *very rare:* indicate respectively smaller populations.

Accidental: far removed from normal range and of extremely rare occurrence.

Irregular or *irregularly:* showing wide fluctuations in appearance or abundance in a given area for comparable seasons in different years.

BIRD PORTRAITS

Plate 1 | LOONS Family Gaviidae
About one-sixth life size

COMMON LOON
Gavia immer

♂

immature ♂ ♀

Fall and winter, and

Common transient visitant.
Rare to fairly common summer resident; rare winter resident.

J F M A M J J A S O N D

RED-THROATED LOON
Gavia stellata

♂ ♀

♂ ♀

Fall and winter

Uncommon transient visitant.
Very rare summer visitant; rare to uncommon winter resident.

J F M A M J J A S O N D

2

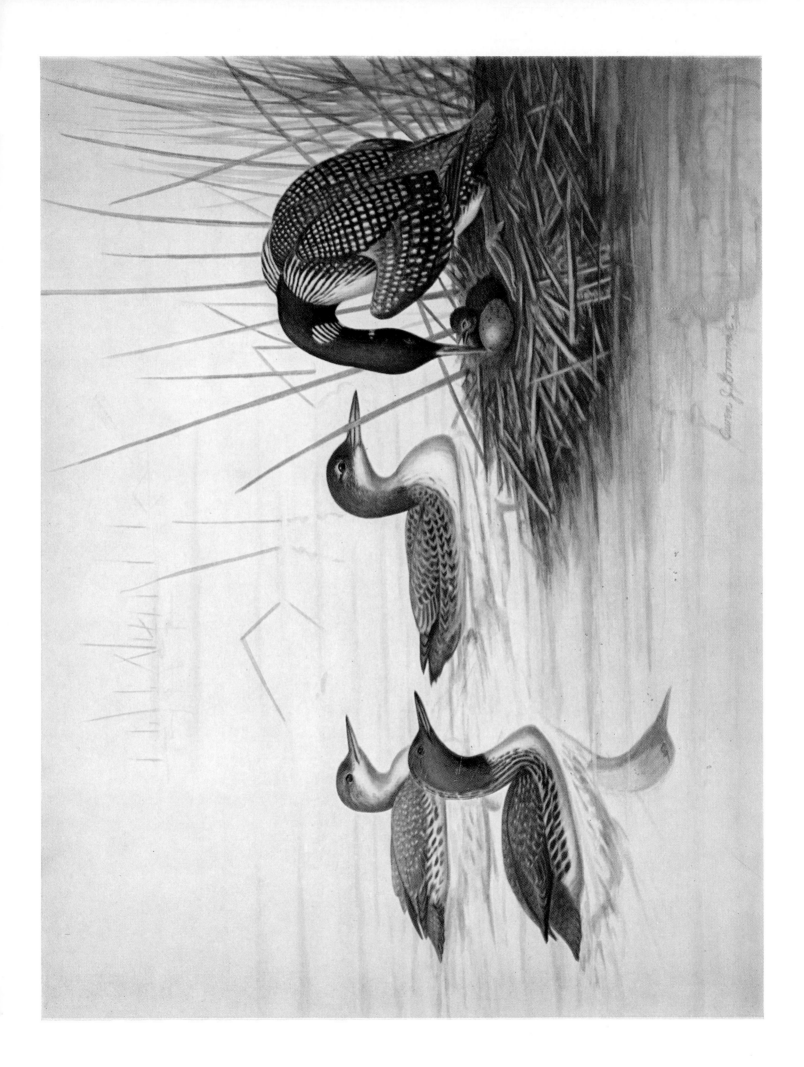

RED-NECKED GREBE
Podiceps grisegena

Fall and winter ♂ ♀

♂ ♀

Rare transient visitant.
Very rare summer resident.

J F M A M J J A S O N D

HORNED GREBE
Podiceps auritus

Fall and winter ♂ ♀

♂ ♀

Fairly common transient visitant.
Rare summer resident; rare winter visitant.

J F M A M J J A S O N D

WESTERN GREBE
Aechmophorus occidentalis

♂ ♀

Uncommon to rare transient visitant.
Very rare winter visitant.

J F M A M J J A S O N D

EARED GREBE
Podiceps caspicus

Fall and winter ♂ ♀

♀

♂

Rare transient visitant.
Very rare summer resident.

J F M A M J J A S O N D

PIED-BILLED GREBE
Podilymbus podiceps

Fall and winter ♂ ♀

♂ ♀

Common transient visitant.
Common to abundant summer resident; rare winter resident.

J F M A M J J A S O N D

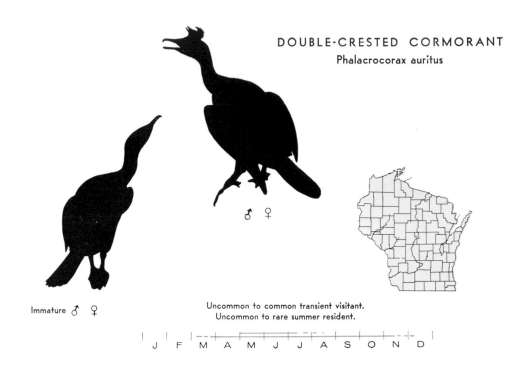

DOUBLE-CRESTED CORMORANT
Phalacrocorax auritus

Immature ♂ ♀

Uncommon to common transient visitant.
Uncommon to rare summer resident.

J F M A M J J A S O N D

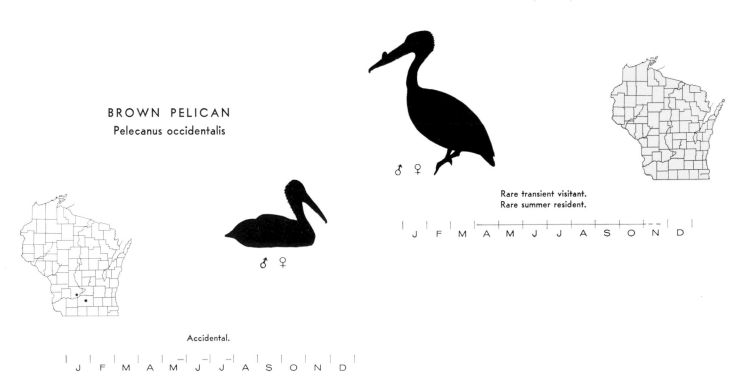

WHITE PELICAN
Pelecanus erythrorhynchos

BROWN PELICAN
Pelecanus occidentalis

♂ ♀

Rare transient visitant.
Rare summer resident.

J F M A M J J A S O N D

Accidental.

J F M A M J J A S O N D

COMMON EGRET
Casmerodius albus

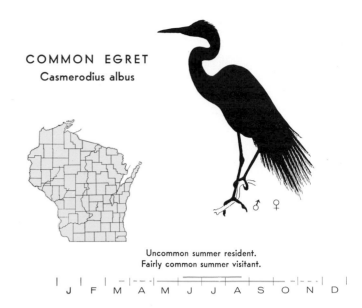

Uncommon summer resident.
Fairly common summer visitant.

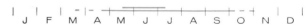

J F M A M J J A S O N D

BLACK-CROWNED NIGHT HERON
Nycticorax nycticorax

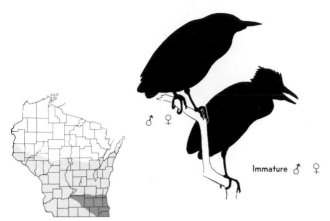

Immature ♂ ♀

Common transient visitant.
Common summer resident locally; rare winter resident.

J F M A M J J A S O N D

GREEN HERON
Butorides virescens

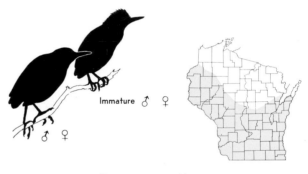

Immature ♂ ♀

♀

Common summer resident.

J F M A M J J A S O N D

YELLOW-CROWNED NIGHT HERON
Nyctanassa violacea

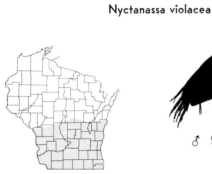

♂ ♀

Rare summer resident.

J F M A M J J A S O N D

LITTLE BLUE HERON
Florida caerulea

See plate 89

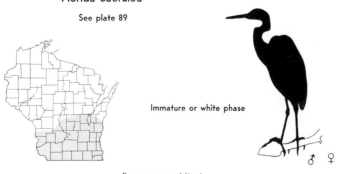

Immature or white phase

♂ ♀

Rare summer visitant.

J F M A M J J A S O N D

SNOWY EGRET
Leucophoyx thula

♂ ♀

Rare summer visitant.

J F M A M J J A S O N D

9

GLOSSY IBIS
Plegadis falcinellus

Immature ♂ ♀

Very rare summer visitant.

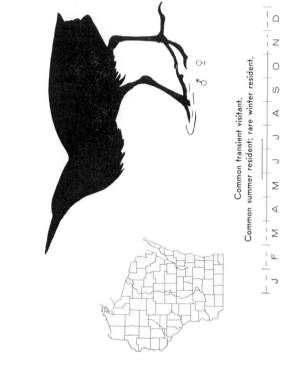

AMERICAN BITTERN
Botaurus lentiginosus

♂ ♀

Common transient visitant.
Common summer resident; rare winter resident.

WOOD IBIS
Mycteria americana

♀
♂

Accidental.

LEAST BITTERN
Ixobrychus exilis

♂ ♀

Fairly common summer resident.

Swans about one-twelfth life size
Geese and brant about one-eighth life size

WHISTLING SWAN
Olor columbianus

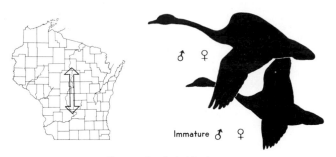

Common transient visitant.

J F M A M J J A S O N D

CANADA GOOSE
Branta canadensis

Common transient visitant.
Uncommon summer resident; uncommon to common winter resident.

J F M A M J J A S O N D

(RICHARDSON'S) CANADA GOOSE
Branta canadensis

See Canada Goose.

♂ ♀

SNOW GOOSE
Chen hyperborea

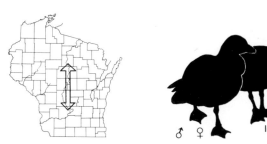

Immature ♂ ♀

Fairly common transient visitant in fall.
Uncommon transient visitant in spring; very rare winter resident.

J F M A M J J A S O N D

WHITE-FRONTED GOOSE
Anser albifrons

Rare transient visitant.

J F M A M J J A S O N D

BLUE GOOSE
Chen caerulescens

♂ ♀

Fairly common transient visitant in fall.
Uncommon transient visitant in spring; very rare winter resident.

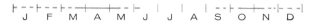

J F M A M J J A S O N D

BRANT
Branta bernicla

♂ ♀

Very rare transient visitant.

J F M A M J J A S O N D

MALLARD
Anas platyrhynchos

BLACK DUCK
Anas rubripes

♂ ♀

Common transient visitant.
Fairly common summer resident; fairly common winter resident.

J F M A M J J A S O N D

Abundant transient visitant.
Common summer resident; fairly common winter resident.

J F M A M J J A S O N D

AMERICAN WIDGEON
Mareca americana

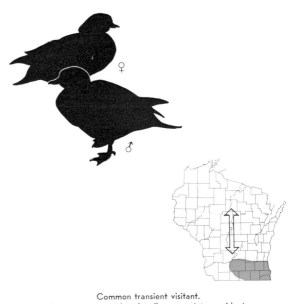

EUROPEAN WIDGEON
Mareca penelope

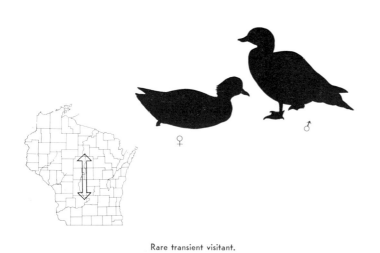

♀

Rare transient visitant.

J F M A M J J A S O N D

Common transient visitant.
Rare summer resident locally; rare winter resident.

J F M A M J J A S O N D

14

Owen J. Gromme.

GADWALL
Anas strepera

Fairly common transient visitant.
Rare summer resident locally; rare winter resident.

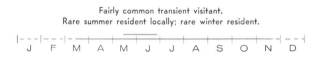
J F M A M J J A S O N D

GREEN-WINGED TEAL
Anas carolinensis

Fairly common transient visitant.
Uncommon summer resident; rare winter resident.

J F M A M J J A S O N D

BLUE-WINGED TEAL
Anas discors

Abundant transient visitant.
Common summer resident; very rare winter resident.

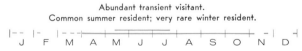
J F M A M J J A S O N D

CINNAMON TEAL
Anas cyanoptera

Accidental.

J F M A M J J A S O N D

PINTAIL
Anas acuta

Common transient visitant.
Uncommon summer resident; rare winter resident.

J F M A M J J A S O N D

WOOD DUCK
Aix sponsa

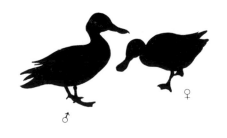

SHOVELER
Spatula clypeata

Fairly common transient visitant.
Fairly common summer resident; very rare winter resident.

J F M A M J J A S O N D

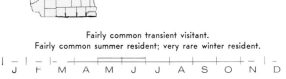

Fairly common transient visitant.
Uncommon summer resident; rare winter resident.

J F M A M J J A S O N D

18

GREATER SCAUP
Aythya marila

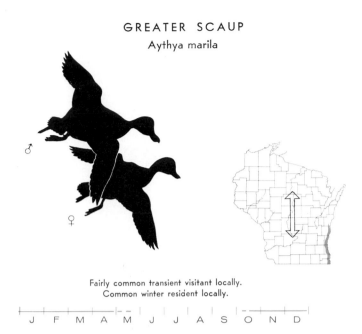

Fairly common transient visitant locally.
Common winter resident locally.

J F M A M J J A S O N D

REDHEAD
Aythya americana

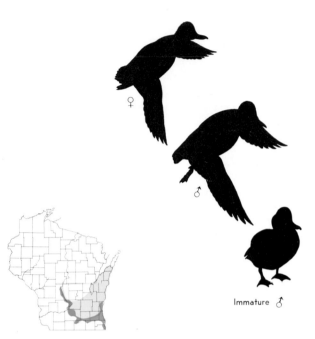

Immature ♂

Fairly common transient visitant.
Uncommon summer resident locally; rare winter resident.

J F M A M J J A S O N D

CANVASBACK
Aythya valisineria

Fairly common transient visitant.
Rare summer resident; uncommon winter resident.

J F M A M J J A S O N D

LESSER SCAUP
Aythya affinis

RING-NECKED DUCK
Aythya collaris

Common transient visitant.
Uncommon summer resident; rare winter resident.

J F M A M J J A S O N D

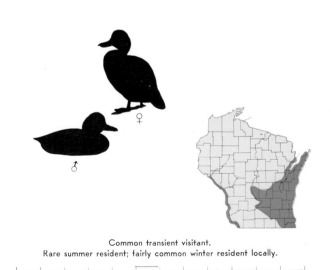

Common transient visitant.
Rare summer resident; fairly common winter resident locally.

J F M A M J J A S O N D

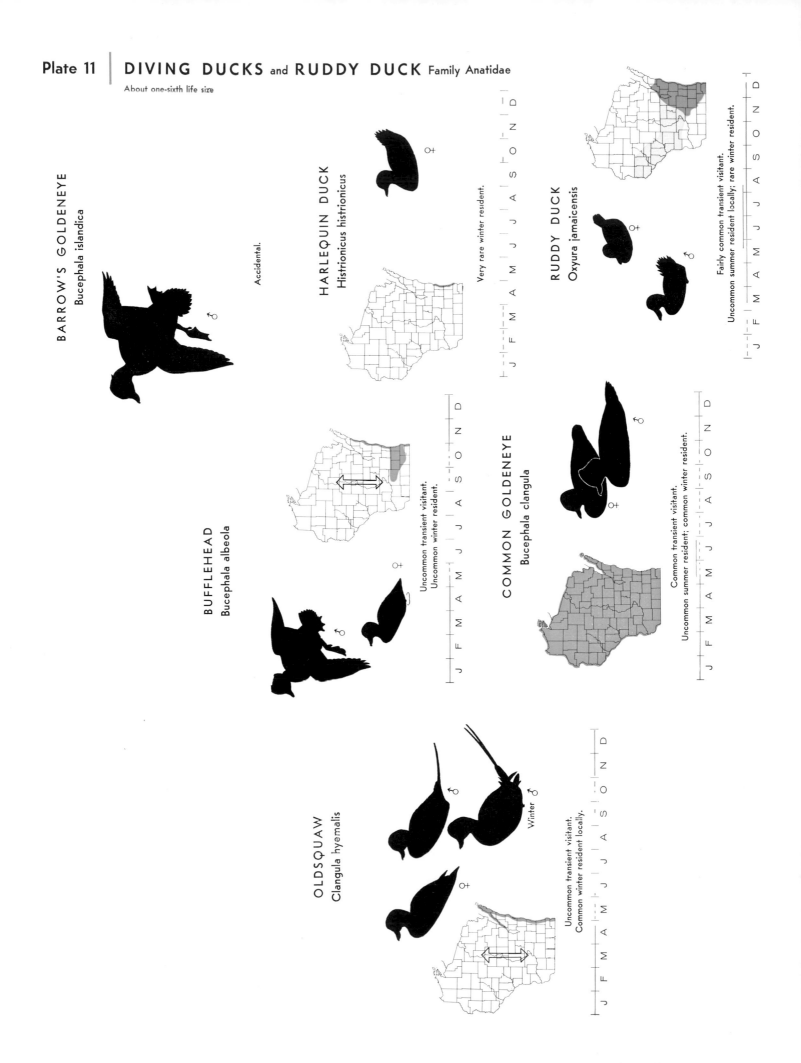

BARROW'S GOLDENEYE
Bucephala islandica

Accidental.

HARLEQUIN DUCK
Histrionicus histrionicus

Very rare winter resident.

RUDDY DUCK
Oxyura jamaicensis

Fairly common transient visitant.
Uncommon summer resident locally; rare winter resident.

BUFFLEHEAD
Bucephala albeola

Uncommon transient visitant.
Uncommon winter resident.

COMMON GOLDENEYE
Bucephala clangula

Common transient visitant.
Uncommon summer resident; common winter resident.

OLDSQUAW
Clangula hyemalis

Winter ♂

Uncommon transient visitant.
Common winter resident locally.

24

COMMON SCOTER
Oidemia nigra

♀

♂

Rare transient visitant.

J F M A M J J A S O N D

KING EIDER
Somateria spectabilis

♀

♂

Very rare winter visitant.

J F M A M J J A S O N D

WHITE-WINGED SCOTER
Melanitta deglandi

♀

♂

Uncommon transient visitant.
Uncommon winter resident.

J F M A M J J A S O N D

SURF SCOTER
Melanitta perspicillata

♀

♂

Rare transient visitant.

J F M A M J J A S O N D

Plate 13 | **MERGANSERS** Family Anatidae

About one-sixth life size

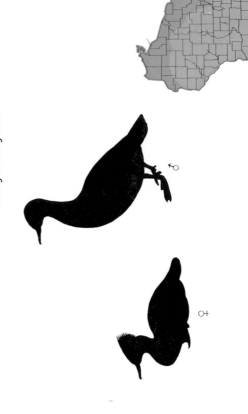

HOODED MERGANSER
Lophodytes cucullatus

♀

♂

Fairly common transient visitant.
Uncommon summer resident; rare winter resident.

J F M A M J J A S O N D

COMMON MERGANSER
Mergus merganser

♂

♀

Common transient visitant.
Uncommon summer resident locally; common winter resident locally.

J F M A M J J A S O N D

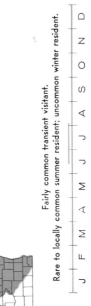

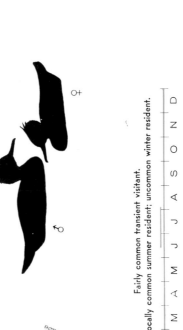

♀

♂

RED-BREASTED MERGANSER
Mergus serrator

Fairly common transient visitant.
Rare to locally common summer resident; uncommon winter resident.

J F M A M J J A S O N D

BLACK VULTURE
Coragyps atratus

FERRUGINOUS HAWK
Buteo regalis

TURKEY VULTURE
Cathartes aura

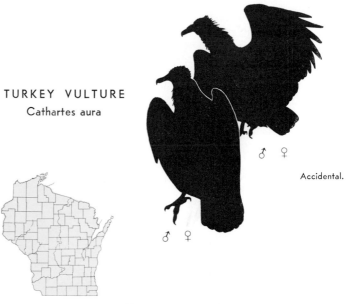

♂ ♀

Accidental.

Very rare transient visitant.

J F M A M J J A S O N D

ROUGH-LEGGED HAWK
Buteo lagopus

Light phase

♂ ♀

Dark phase

♂ ♀

Uncommon transient visitant.
Uncommon summer resident.

J F M A M J J A S O N D

MARSH HAWK
Circus cyaneus

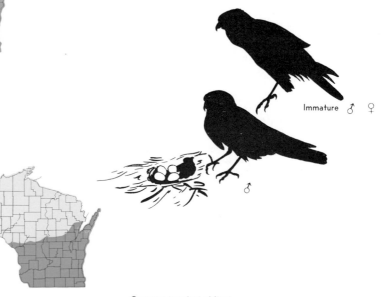

Immature ♂ ♀

♂

Fairly common transient visitant.
Fairly common winter resident.

J F M A M J J A S O N D

Common transient visitant.
Common summer resident; uncommon winter resident.

J F M A M J J A S O N D

Plate 15 │ **BIRD HAWKS** Family Accipitridae

About one-fourth life size

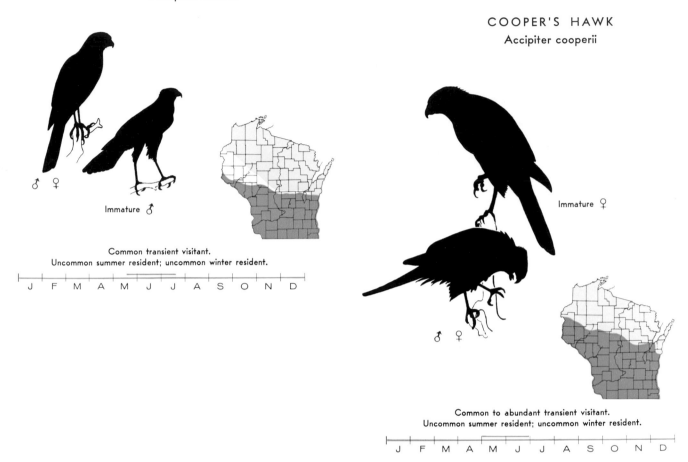

SHARP-SHINNED HAWK
Accipiter striatus

♂ ♀

Immature ♂

Common transient visitant.
Uncommon summer resident; uncommon winter resident.

J F M A M J J A S O N D

COOPER'S HAWK
Accipiter cooperii

Immature ♀

♂ ♀

Common to abundant transient visitant.
Uncommon summer resident; uncommon winter resident.

J F M A M J J A S O N D

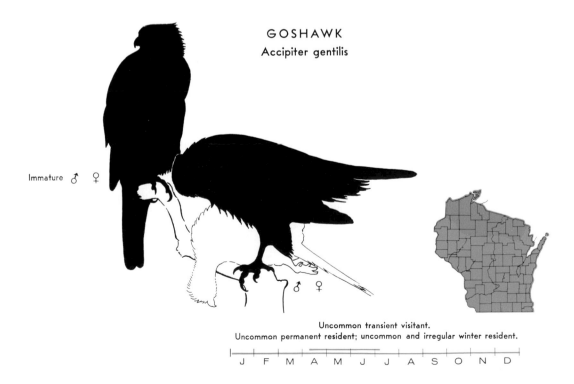

GOSHAWK
Accipiter gentilis

Immature ♂ ♀

♂ ♀

Uncommon transient visitant.
Uncommon permanent resident; uncommon and irregular winter resident.

J F M A M J J A S O N D

(WESTERN) RED-TAILED HAWK
Buteo jamaicensis

♂ ♀

See (Eastern) Red-tailed Hawk.

(EASTERN) RED-TAILED HAWK
Buteo jamaicensis

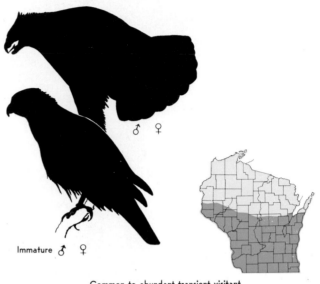

♂ ♀

Immature ♂ ♀

Common to abundant transient visitant.
Common summer resident; fairly common winter resident.

J F M A M J J A S O N D

HARLAN'S HAWK
Buteo harlani

♂ ♀

Very rare transient visitant.

J F M A M J J A S O N D

(KRIDER'S) RED-TAILED HAWK
Buteo jamaicensis

♂ ♀

See (Eastern) Red-tailed Hawk.

Plate 17 | **HAWKS** and **KITE** Family Accipitridae

Hawks about one-fourth life size
Kite about one-eighth life size

SWALLOW-TAILED KITE
Elanoides forficatus

♂ ♀

Accidental.

BROAD-WINGED HAWK
Buteo platypterus

Immature ♂ ♀

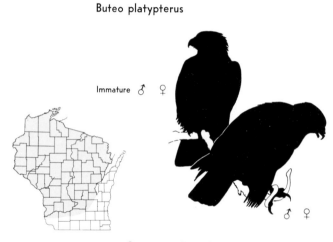

♂ ♀

Common transient visitant.
Rare to fairly common summer resident.

J F M A M J J A S O N D

RED-SHOULDERED HAWK
Buteo lineatus

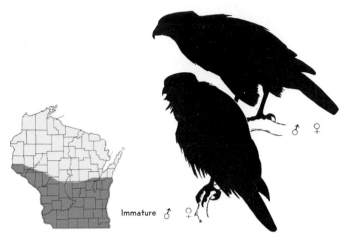

♂ ♀

Immature ♂ ♀

Fairly common transient visitant.
Fairly common summer resident; uncommon winter resident.

J F M A M J J A S O N D

SWAINSON'S HAWK
Buteo swainsoni

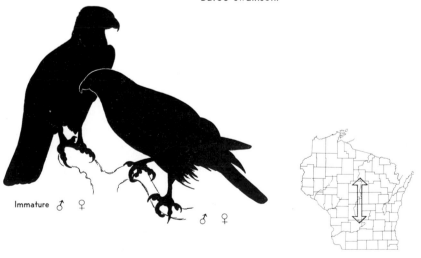

Immature ♂ ♀

♂ ♀

Rare transient visitant.

J F M A M J J A S O N D

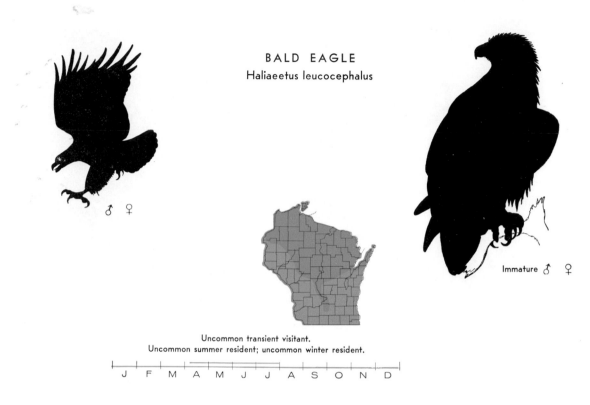

BALD EAGLE
Haliaeetus leucocephalus

♂ ♀

Immature ♂ ♀

Uncommon transient visitant.
Uncommon summer resident; uncommon winter resident.

J F M A M J J A S O N D

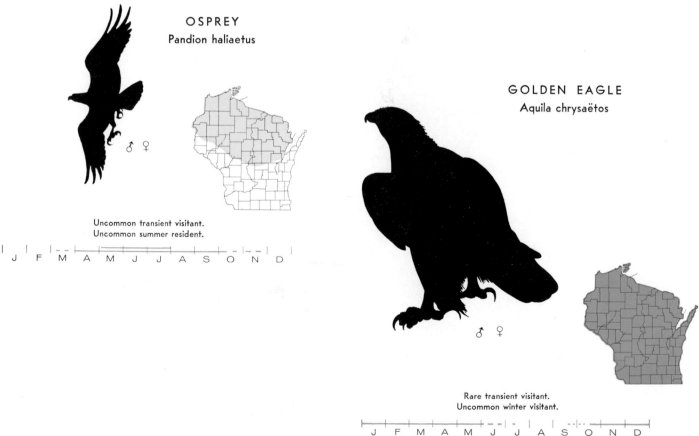

OSPREY
Pandion haliaetus

♂ ♀

Uncommon transient visitant.
Uncommon summer resident.

J F M A M J J A S O N D

GOLDEN EAGLE
Aquila chrysaëtos

♂ ♀

Rare transient visitant.
Uncommon winter visitant.

J F M A M J J A S O N D

Plate 19 | FALCONS Family Falconidae

About one-third life size

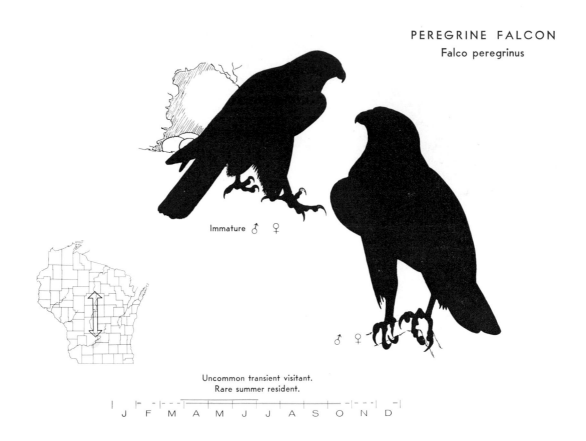

PEREGRINE FALCON
Falco peregrinus

Immature ♂ ♀

♂ ♀

Uncommon transient visitant.
Rare summer resident.

J F M A M J J A S O N D

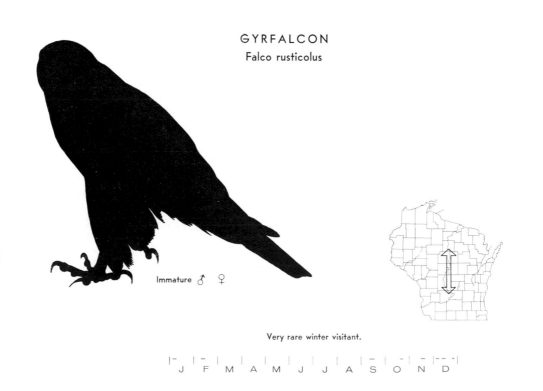

GYRFALCON
Falco rusticolus

Immature ♂ ♀

Very rare winter visitant.

J F M A M J J A S O N D

38

Owen J. Gromme.

39

SPARROW HAWK
Falco sparverius

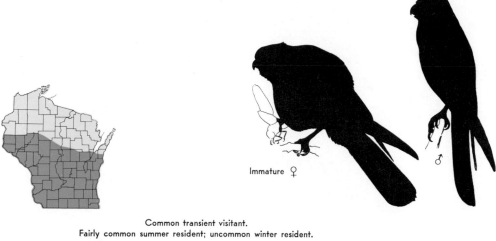

Immature ♀

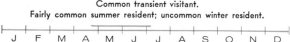

Common transient visitant.
Fairly common summer resident; uncommon winter resident.

J F M A M J J A S O N D

PIGEON HAWK
Falco columbarius

Immature ♀

Fairly common transient visitant.
Rare summer visitant; rare winter resident.

J F M A M J J A S O N D

Plate 21 | GROUSE Family Tetraonidae
About one-third life size

SPRUCE GROUSE
Canachites canadensis

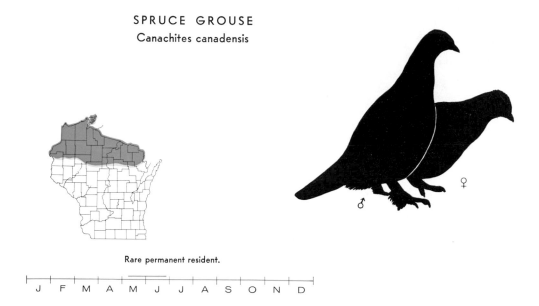

Rare permanent resident.

J F M A M J J A S O N D

RUFFED GROUSE
Bonasa umbellus

Red phase ♂ ♀

Gray phase ♂ ♀

Common permanent resident.

J F M A M J J A S O N D

42

SHARP-TAILED GROUSE
Pedioecetes phasianellus

Dancing males

○♀

Formerly an abundant resident locally. Now drastically reduced
numbers occur in isolated areas. Future uncertain.

J F M A M J J A S O N D

GREATER PRAIRIE CHICKEN
Tympanuchus cupido

Dancing males

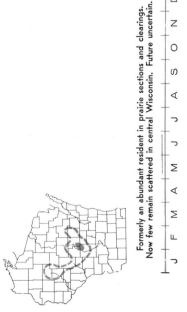

○♀

Formerly an abundant resident in prairie sections and clearings.
Now few remain scattered in central Wisconsin. Future uncertain.

J F M A M J J A S O N D

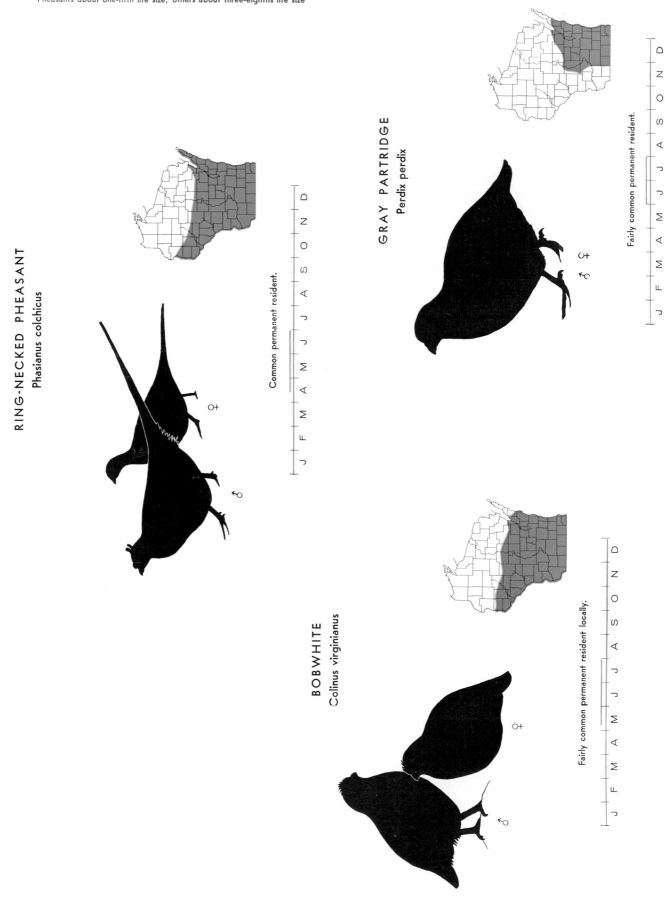

RING-NECKED PHEASANT
Phasianus colchicus

Common permanent resident.

J F M A M J J A S O N D

GRAY PARTRIDGE
Perdix perdix

Fairly common permanent resident.

J F M A M J J A S O N D

BOBWHITE
Colinus virginianus

Fairly common permanent resident locally.

J F M A M J J A S O N D

TURKEY
Meleagris gallopavo

Immature ♂

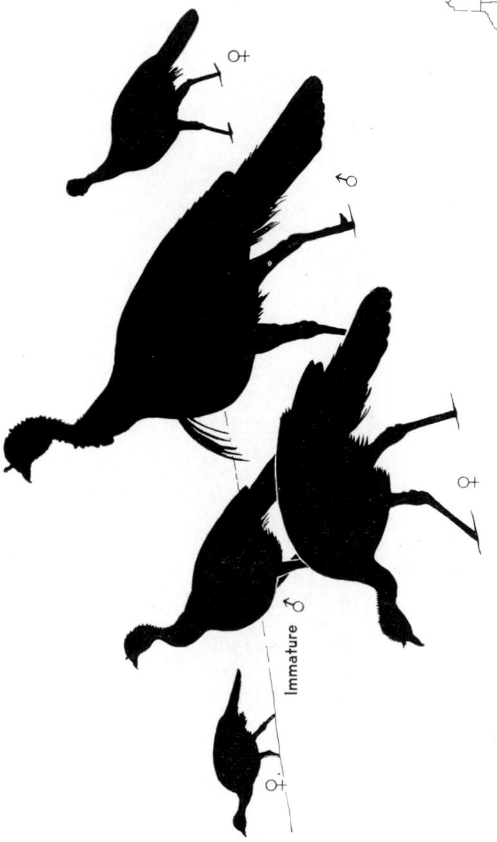

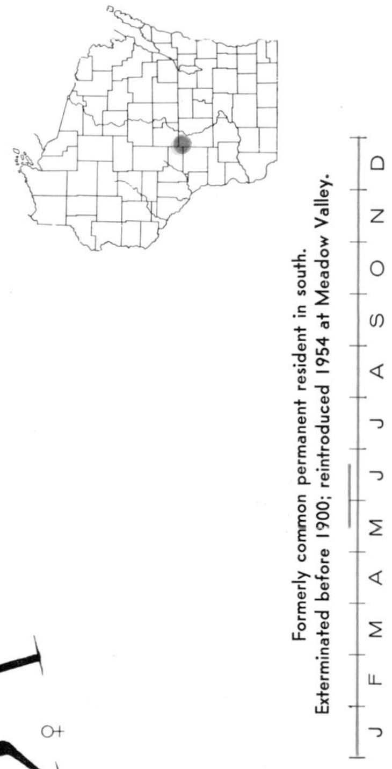

Formerly common permanent resident in south.
Exterminated before 1900; reintroduced 1954 at Meadow Valley.

J F M A M J J A S O N D

GREAT BLUE HERON
Ardea herodias

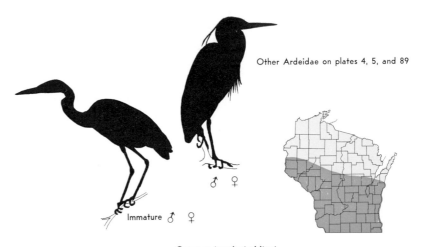

Other Ardeidae on plates 4, 5, and 89

Immature ♂ ♀

Common transient visitant.
Fairly common summer resident; rare winter resident.

J F M A M J J A S O N D

WHOOPING CRANE
Grus americana

Formerly uncommon; now nearly extinct.

SANDHILL CRANE
Grus canadensis

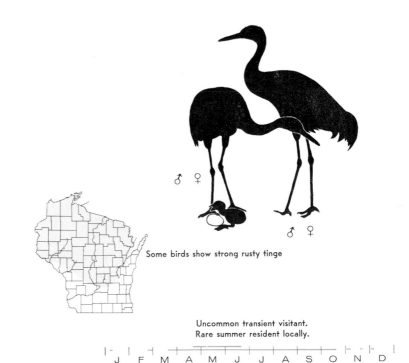

Some birds show strong rusty tinge

Uncommon transient visitant.
Rare summer resident locally.

J F M A M J J A S O N D

50

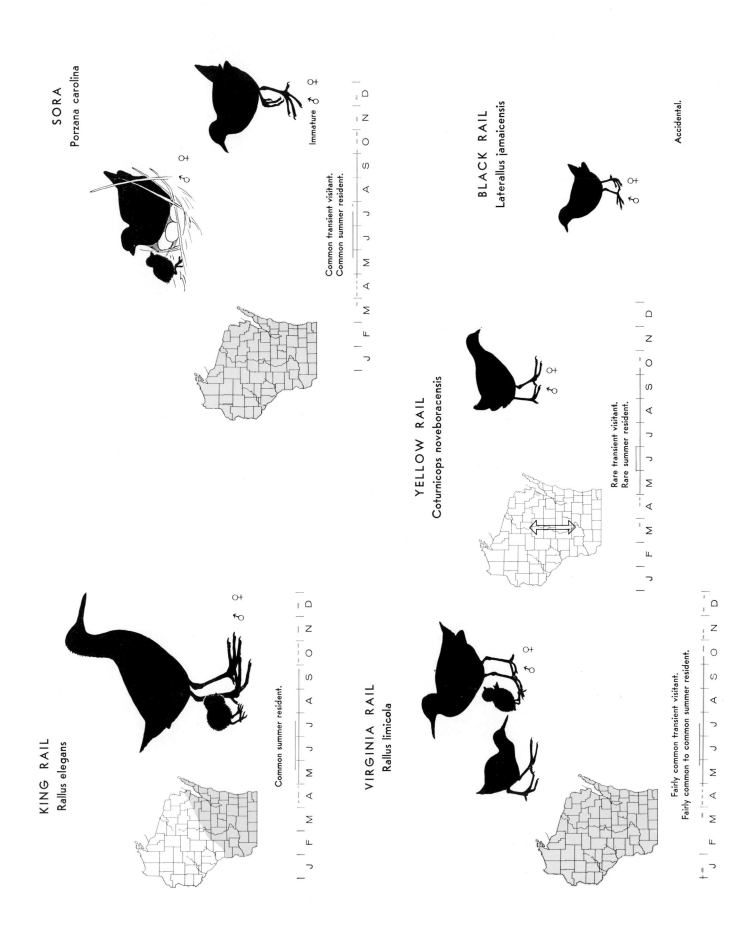

SORA
Porzana carolina

Immature ♂ ♀

♀

♂

Common transient visitant.
Common summer resident.

J F M A M J J A S O N D

KING RAIL
Rallus elegans

♀

♂

Common summer resident.

J F M A M J J A S O N D

YELLOW RAIL
Coturnicops noveboracensis

♀

♂

Rare transient visitant.
Rare summer resident.

J F M A M J J A S O N D

BLACK RAIL
Laterallus jamaicensis

♀

♂

Accidental.

J F M A M J J A S O N D

VIRGINIA RAIL
Rallus limicola

♀

♂

Fairly common transient visitant.
Fairly common to common summer resident.

J F M A M J J A S O N D

Plate 27

GALLINULE and COOT Family Rallidae

AMERICAN AVOCET Family Recurvirostridae

All about one-fourth life size

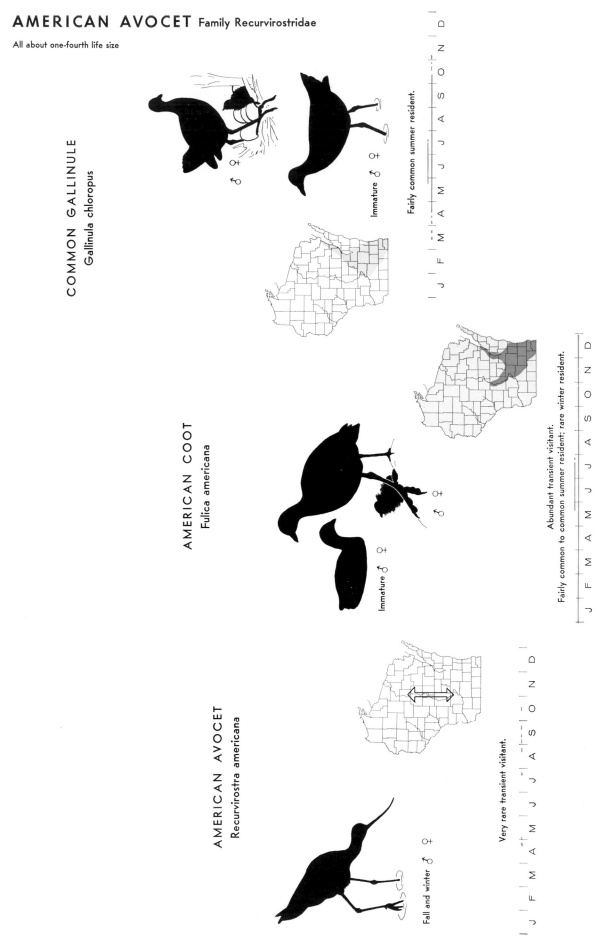

COMMON GALLINULE
Gallinula chloropus

Immature ♂ ♀

Fairly common summer resident.

J F M A M J J A S O N D

AMERICAN COOT
Fulica americana

Immature ♂ ♀

Abundant transient visitant.
Fairly common to common summer resident; rare winter resident.

J F M A M J J A S O N D

AMERICAN AVOCET
Recurvirostra americana

Fall and winter ♂ ♀

Very rare transient visitant.

J F M A M J J A S O N D

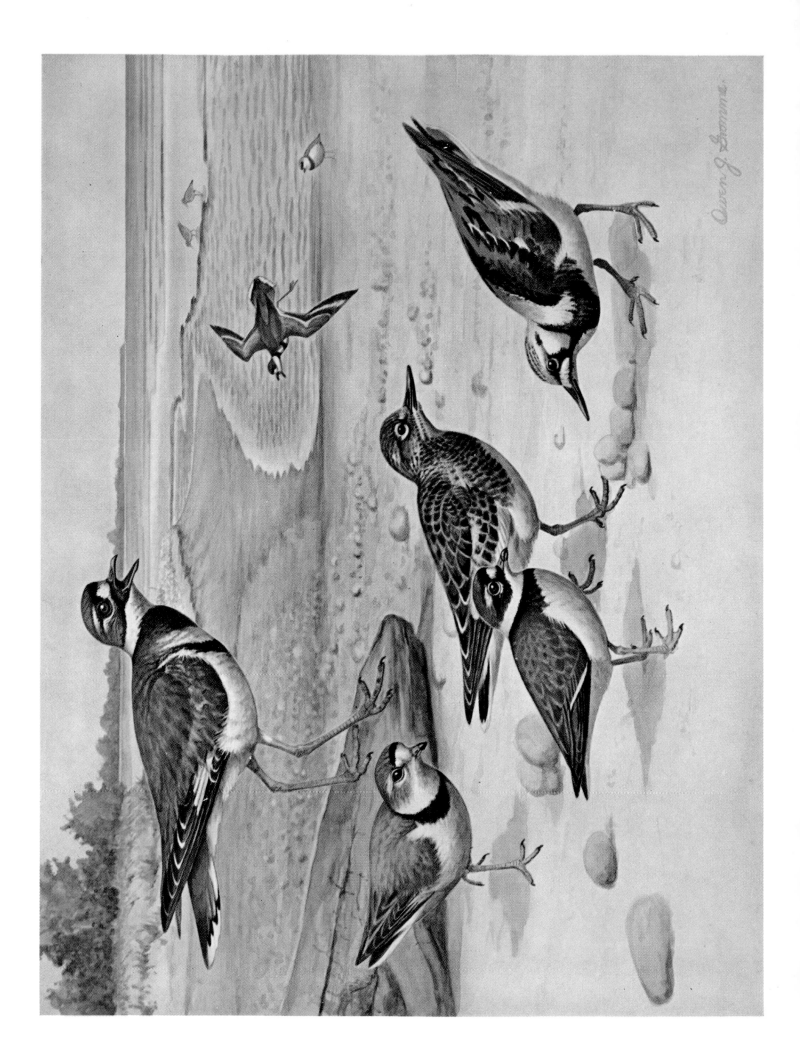

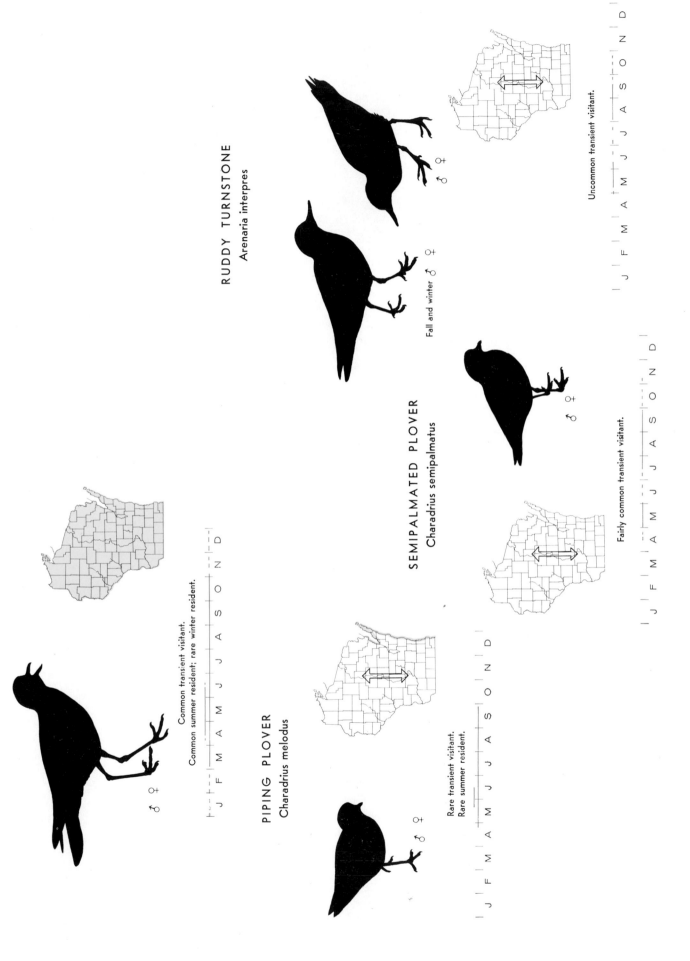

RUDDY TURNSTONE
Arenaria interpres

Fall and winter ♂ ♀

♂ ♀

Uncommon transient visitant.

J F M A M J J A S O N D

KILLDEER
Charadrius vociferus

♂

Common transient visitant.
Common summer resident; rare winter resident.

J F M A M J J A S O N D

SEMIPALMATED PLOVER
Charadrius semipalmatus

♂ ♀

Fairly common transient visitant.

J F M A M J J A S O N D

PIPING PLOVER
Charadrius melodus

♂ ♀

Rare transient visitant.
Rare summer resident.

J F M A M J J A S O N D

AMERICAN GOLDEN PLOVER
Pluvialis dominica

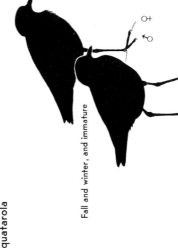

Fall and winter, and immature

♀

♂

♀

♂

Uncommon transient visitant.

J F M A M J J A S O N D

UPLAND PLOVER
Bartramia longicauda

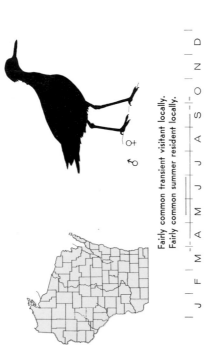

♀

♂

Fairly common transient visitant locally.
Fairly common summer resident locally.

J F M A M J J A S O N D

BLACK-BELLIED PLOVER
Squatarola squatarola

♀

♂

♀

♂

Fall and winter, and immature

Fairly common transient visitant.

J F M A M J J A S O N D

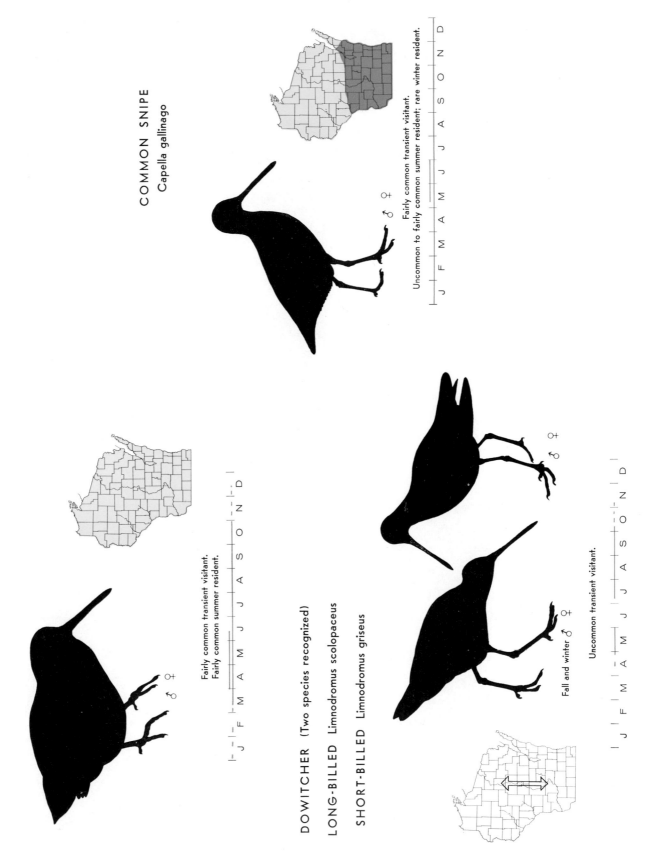

COMMON SNIPE
Capella gallinago

Uncommon to fairly common summer resident; rare winter resident.
Fairly common transient visitant.

♂ ♀

J F M A M J J A S O N D

AMERICAN WOODCOCK
Philohela minor

Fairly common transient visitant.
Fairly common summer resident.

♀
♂

J F M A M J J A S O N D

DOWITCHER (Two species recognized)
LONG-BILLED *Limnodromus scolopaceus*
SHORT-BILLED *Limnodromus griseus*

♀
♂

Fall and winter ♂ ♀

Uncommon transient visitant.

J F M A M J J A S O N D

61

Plate 31 | **SANDPIPERS** Family Scolopacidae
About one-fourth life size

LONG-BILLED CURLEW
Numenius americanus

♂ ♀

Accidental.

WHIMBREL
Numenius phaeopus

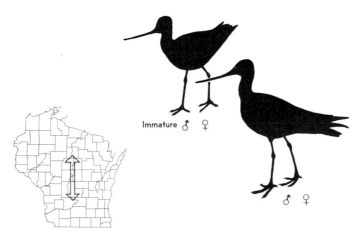

♂ ♀

Rare transient visitant.

J F M A M J J A S O N D

ESKIMO CURLEW
Numenius borealis

♂ ♀

Very rare; long considered extinct.

HUDSONIAN GODWIT
Limosa haemastica

Immature ♂ ♀

♂ ♀

Rare transient visitant.

J F M A M J J A S O N D

MARBLED GODWIT
Limosa fedoa

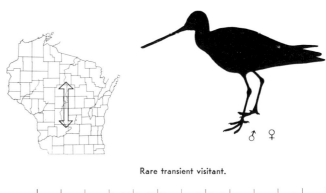

♂ ♀

Rare transient visitant.

J F M A M J J A S O N D

WILLET
Catoptrophorus semipalmatus

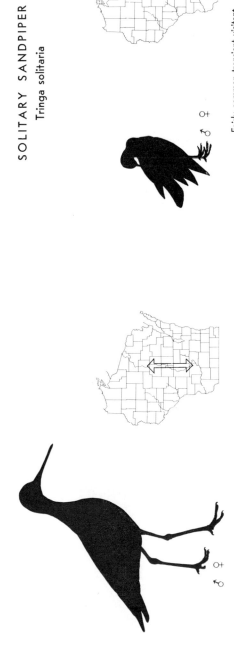

Rare transient visitant.

J F M A M J J A S O N D

SOLITARY SANDPIPER
Tringa solitaria

Fairly common transient visitant.

J F M A M J J A S O N D

SPOTTED SANDPIPER
Actitis macularia

Winter and immature ♂ ♀

Common transient visitant.
Common summer resident.

J F M A M J J A S O N D

GREATER YELLOWLEGS
Totanus melanoleucus

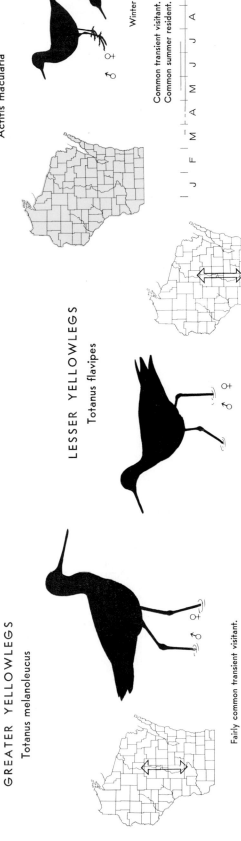

Fairly common transient visitant.

J F M A M J J A S O N D

LESSER YELLOWLEGS
Totanus flavipes

Fairly common transient visitant.

J F M A M J J A S O N D

65

Plate 33 | **SANDPIPERS** Family Scolopacidae

About one-half life size

KNOT
Calidris canutus

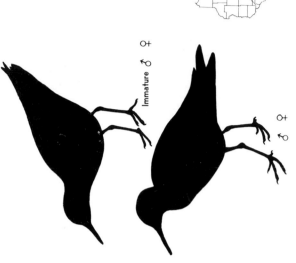

Immature ♂ ♀

♂ ♀

Rare transient visitant.

J F M A M J J A S O N D

PURPLE SANDPIPER
Erolia maritima

Winter ♂ ♀

Accidental.

J F M A M J J A S O N D

STILT SANDPIPER
Micropalama himantopus

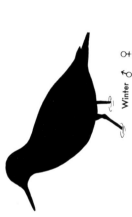

♂ ♀

Fall and winter ♂ ♀

♂ ♀

Uncommon transient visitant.

J F M A M J J A S O N D

WHITE-RUMPED SANDPIPER
Erolia fuscicollis

♀ ♂

Uncommon transient visitant.

J F M A M J J A S O N D

BAIRD'S SANDPIPER
Erolia bairdii

♀ ♂

Uncommon transient visitant.

J F M A M J J A S O N D

SEMIPALMATED SANDPIPER
Ereunetes pusillus

♂ ♀

Common transient visitant.
Uncommon summer resident.

J F M A M J J A S O N D

WESTERN SANDPIPER
Ereunetes mauri

♂ ♀

Rare transient visitant.

J F M A M J J A S O N D

LEAST SANDPIPER
Erolia minutilla

♀

♂

Fairly common transient visitant.

J F M A M J J A S O N D

BUFF-BREASTED SANDPIPER
Tryngites subruficollis

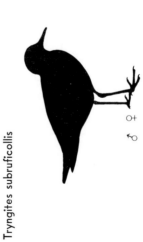

♂

♀

Very rare transient visitant.

J F M A M J J A S O N D

Plate 35 | **SANDPIPERS** Family Scolopacidae

About one-half life size

DUNLIN
Erolia alpina

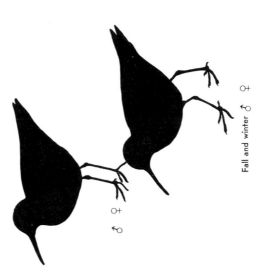

Fall and winter ♂ ♀

♀

♂

Fairly common transient visitant.

J F M A M J J A S O N D

SANDERLING
Crocethia alba

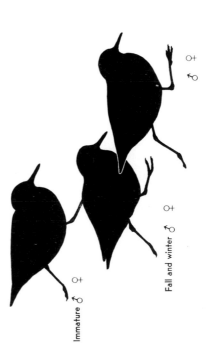

♀

♂

Fall and winter ♂ ♀

♀

Immature ♂

Common transient visitant in east.
Uncommon transient visitant inland.

J F M A M J J A S O N D

PECTORAL SANDPIPER
Erolia melanotos

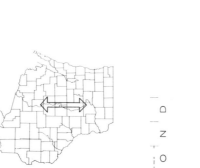

Common transient visitant.
Uncommon summer resident.

J F M A M J J A S O N D

WILSON'S PHALAROPE
Steganopus tricolor

Uncommon transient visitant.
Rare summer resident.

J F M A M J J A S O N D

NORTHERN PHALAROPE
Lobipes lobatus

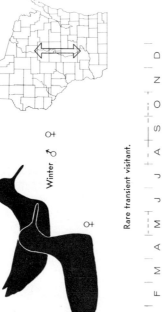

Winter ♂ ♀

♀

Rare transient visitant.

J F M A M J J A S O N D

RED PHALAROPE
Phalaropus fulicarius

♀

Winter ♂ ♀

Very rare transient visitant.

J F M A M J J A S O N D

PARASITIC JAEGER
Stercorarius parasiticus

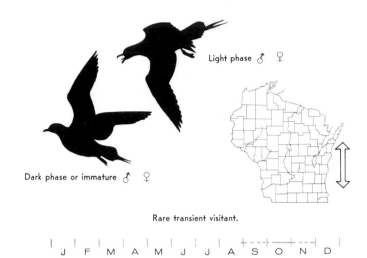

Light phase ♂ ♀

Dark phase or immature ♂ ♀

Rare transient visitant.

| J | F | M | A | M | J | J | A | S | O | N | D |

POMARINE JAEGER
Stercorarius pomarinus

♂ ♀

Accidental.

| J | F | M | A | M | J | J | A | S | O | N | D |

GLAUCOUS GULL
Larus hyperboreus

♂ ♀

Immature ♂ ♀

Rare winter visitant.

| J | F | M | A | M | J | J | A | S | O | N | D |

GREAT BLACK-BACKED GULL
Larus marinus

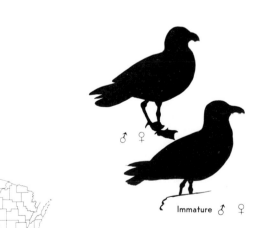

♂ ♀

Immature ♂ ♀

Rare winter visitant.

| J | F | M | A | M | J | J | A | S | O | N | D |

BONAPARTE'S GULL
Larus philadelphia

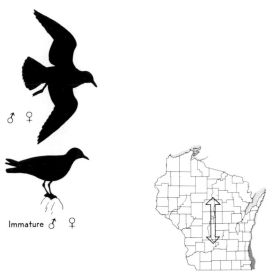

♂ ♀

Immature ♂ ♀

Uncommon to common transient visitant.
Rare to uncommon summer resident; fairly common winter resident.

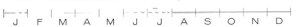

J F M A M J J A S O N D

FRANKLIN'S GULL
Larus pipixcan

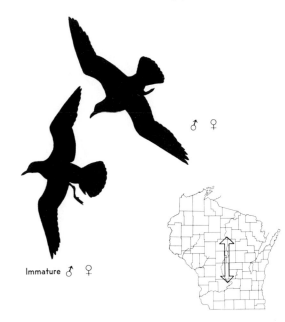

♂ ♀

Immature ♂ ♀

Uncommon transient visitant.

J F M A M J J A S O N D

RING-BILLED GULL
Larus delawarensis

♂ ♀

Immature ♂ ♀

Common transient visitant.
Fairly common summer resident; fairly common winter resident.

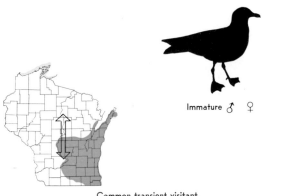

J F M A M J J A S O N D

HERRING GULL
Larus argentatus

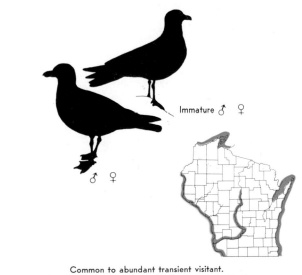

Immature ♂ ♀

♂ ♀

Common to abundant transient visitant.
Common summer resident; abundant winter resident.

J F M A M J J A S O N D

Plate 39 | **TERNS** Family Laridae
About one-fourth life size

ARCTIC TERN
Sterna paradisaea

♂ ♀

Accidental.

COMMON TERN
Sterna hirundo

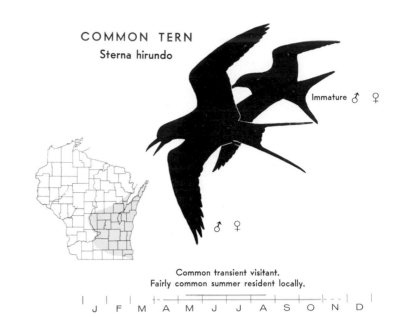

Immature ♂ ♀

♂ ♀

Common transient visitant.
Fairly common summer resident locally.

J F M A M J J A S O N D

CASPIAN TERN
Hydroprogne caspia

Immature ♂ ♀

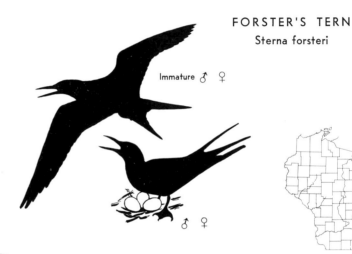

♂ ♀

Uncommon transient visitant.
Rare to common summer resident locally.

J F M A M J J A S O N D

FORSTER'S TERN
Sterna forsteri

Immature ♂ ♀

♂ ♀

Uncommon transient visitant.
Uncommon summer resident locally.

J F M A M J J A S O N D

BLACK TERN
Chlidonias niger

Late summer ♂ ♀

♂ ♀

Common transient visitant.
Common to abundant summer resident.

J F M A M J J A S O N D

LEAST TERN
Sterna albifrons

♂ ♀   Immature ♂ ♀

Accidental.

J F M A M J J A S O N D

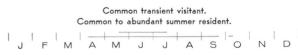

PASSENGER PIGEON
Ectopistes migratorius

♀

♂

Extinct.

MOURNING DOVE
Zenaidura macroura

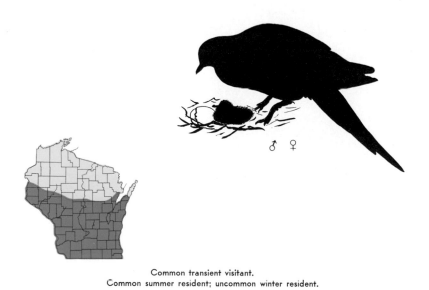

♂ ♀

Common transient visitant.
Common summer resident; uncommon winter resident.

|–|–·–|–|–|———| - - - - - - - - |–|–·–|–·–|–|
J F M A M J J A S O N D

YELLOW-BILLED CUCKOO
Coccyzus americanus

BLACK-BILLED CUCKOO
Coccyzus erythropthalmus

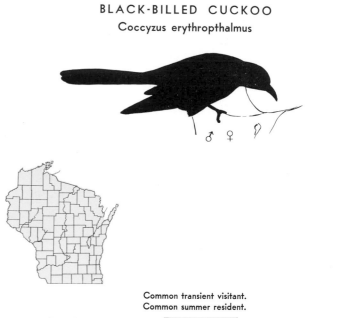

Common transient visitant.
Common summer resident.

J F M A M J J A S O N D

Uncommon to fairly common transient visitant.
Uncommon to fairly common summer resident.

J F M A M J J A S O N D

BELTED KINGFISHER
Megaceryle alcyon

Fairly common transient visitant.
Fairly common summer resident; uncommon winter resident.

J F M A M J J A S O N D

Owen J. Gromme.

83

Owen J. Gromme

LONG-EARED OWL
Asio otus

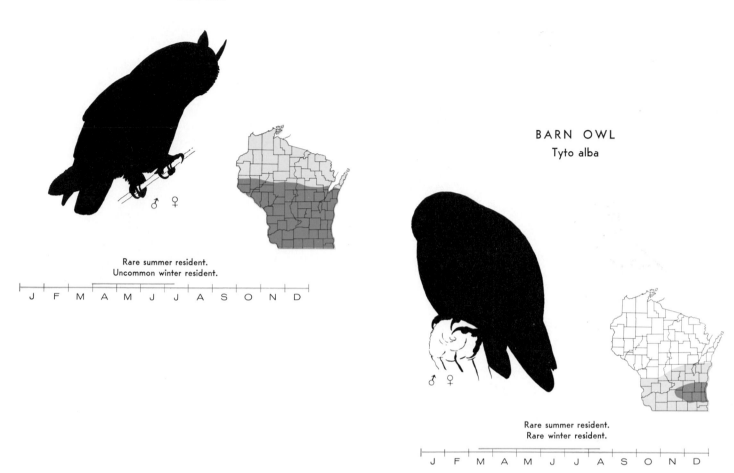

Rare summer resident.
Uncommon winter resident.

J F M A M J J A S O N D

BARN OWL
Tyto alba

Rare summer resident.
Rare winter resident.

J F M A M J J A S O N D

SHORT-EARED OWL
Asio flammeus

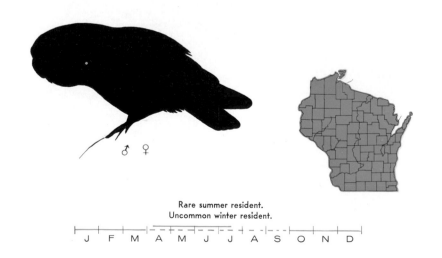

Rare summer resident.
Uncommon winter resident.

J F M A M J J A S O N D

Plate 43 | TYPICAL OWLS Family Strigidae
About one-third life size

HAWK OWL
Surnia ulula

♂ ♀

Very rare winter visitant.

J F M A M J J A S O N D

BOREAL OWL
Aegolius funereus

♂ ♀

Rare winter visitant.

J F M A M J J A S O N D

SCREECH OWL
Otus asio

Gray phase ♂ ♀

Red phase ♂ ♀

Uncommon permanent resident.

J F M A M J J A S O N D

SAW-WHET OWL
Aegolius acadicus

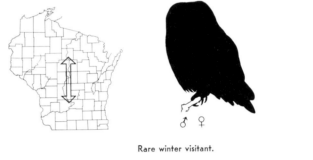

Immature ♂ ♀

♂ ♀

Rare summer resident.
Uncommon winter resident.

J F M A M J J A S O N D

Owen J. Gromme.

BARRED OWL
Strix varia

Fairly common permanent resident.

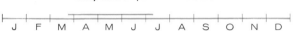

GREAT GRAY OWL
Strix nebulosa

Rare before 1900; no recent records.

SNOWY OWL
Nyctea scandiaca

Uncommon winter resident or visitant; irregular.

GREAT HORNED OWL
Bubo virginianus

Common permanent resident.

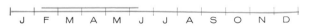

89

CHIMNEY SWIFT
Chaetura pelagica

Female nighthawks flying

Common transient visitant.
Common summer resident.

J F M A M J J A S O N D

WHIP-POOR-WILL
Caprimulgus vociferus

COMMON NIGHTHAWK
Chordeiles minor

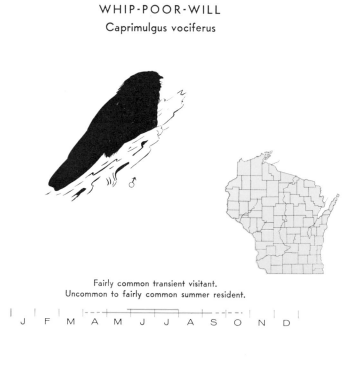

Fairly common transient visitant.
Uncommon to fairly common summer resident.

J F M A M J J A S O N D

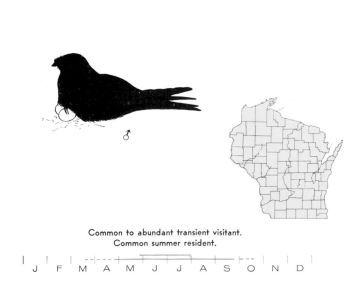

Common to abundant transient visitant.
Common summer resident.

J F M A M J J A S O N D

♂

♀

RUBY-THROATED HUMMINGBIRD
Archilochus colubris

Immature ♂

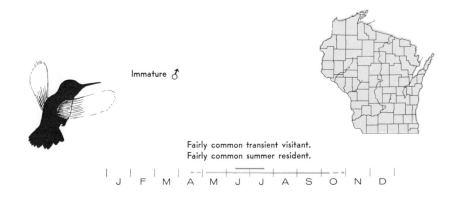

Fairly common transient visitant.
Fairly common summer resident.

J F M A M J J A S O N D

Two-lined Morning Sphinx Moth

Plate 47 | WOODPECKERS Family Picidae
About one-half life size

RED-HEADED WOODPECKER
Melanerpes erythrocephalus

♂ ♀

Immature ♂ ♀

Common transient visitant.
Common summer resident; uncommon winter resident.

J F M A M J J A S O N D

RED-BELLIED WOODPECKER
Centurus carolinus

♂

♀

Fairly common permanent resident.

J F M A M J J A S O N D

YELLOW-SHAFTED FLICKER
Colaptes auratus

♀

♂

Common transient visitant.
Common summer resident; uncommon winter resident or visitant.

J F M A M J J A S O N D

PILEATED WOODPECKER
Dryocopus pileatus

Rare to uncommon permanent resident.

J F M A M J J A S O N D

97

Plate 49 | WOODPECKERS Family Picidae
About one-half life size

DOWNY WOODPECKER
Dendrocopos pubescens

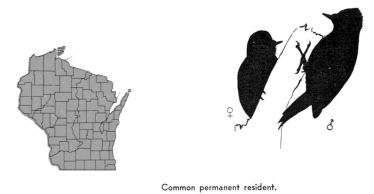

Common permanent resident.

HAIRY WOODPECKER
Dendrocopos villosus

YELLOW-BELLIED SAPSUCKER
Sphyrapicus varius

Common permanent resident.

Common transient visitant.
Fairly common summer resident; rare winter resident.

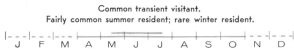

Owen J. Gromme

NORTHERN THREE-TOED WOODPECKER
Picoides tridactylus

Very rare.

J F M A M J J A S O N D

BLACK-BACKED THREE-TOED WOODPECKER
Picoides arcticus

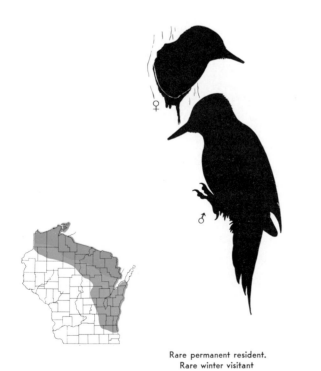

Rare permanent resident.
Rare winter visitant

J F M A M J J A S O N D

GREAT CRESTED FLYCATCHER
Myiarchus crinitus

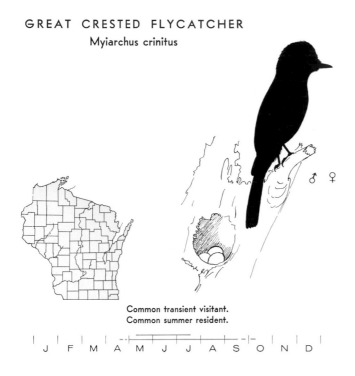

Common transient visitant.
Common summer resident.

J F M A M J J A S O N D

EASTERN KINGBIRD
Tyrannus tyrannus

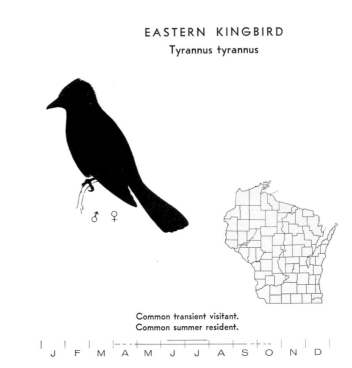

Common transient visitant.
Common summer resident.

J F M A M J J A S O N D

WESTERN KINGBIRD
Tyrannus verticalis

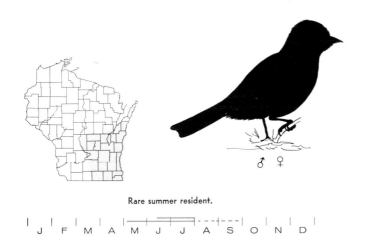

Rare summer resident.

J F M A M J J A S O N D

OLIVE-SIDED FLYCATCHER
Nuttallornis borealis

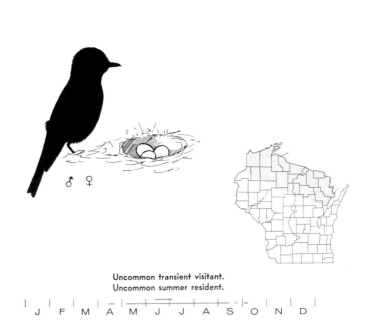

Uncommon transient visitant.
Uncommon summer resident.

J F M A M J J A S O N D

LEAST FLYCATCHER
Empidonax minimus

Common transient visitant.
Fairly common summer resident.

J F M A M J J A S O N D

TRAILL'S FLYCATCHER
Empidonax traillii

Fairly common transient visitant.
Fairly common summer resident.

J F M A M J J A S O N D

EASTERN PHOEBE
Sayornis phoebe

Common transient visitant.
Common summer resident.

J F M A M J J A S O N D

EASTERN WOOD PEWEE
Contopus virens

Common transient visitant.
Common summer resident.

J F M A M J J A S O N D

YELLOW-BELLIED FLYCATCHER
Empidonax flaviventris

Uncommon transient visitant.
Rare summer resident.

J F M A M J J A S O N D

ACADIAN FLYCATCHER
Empidonax virescens

Uncommon transient visitant.
Uncommon summer resident.

J F M A M J J A S O N D

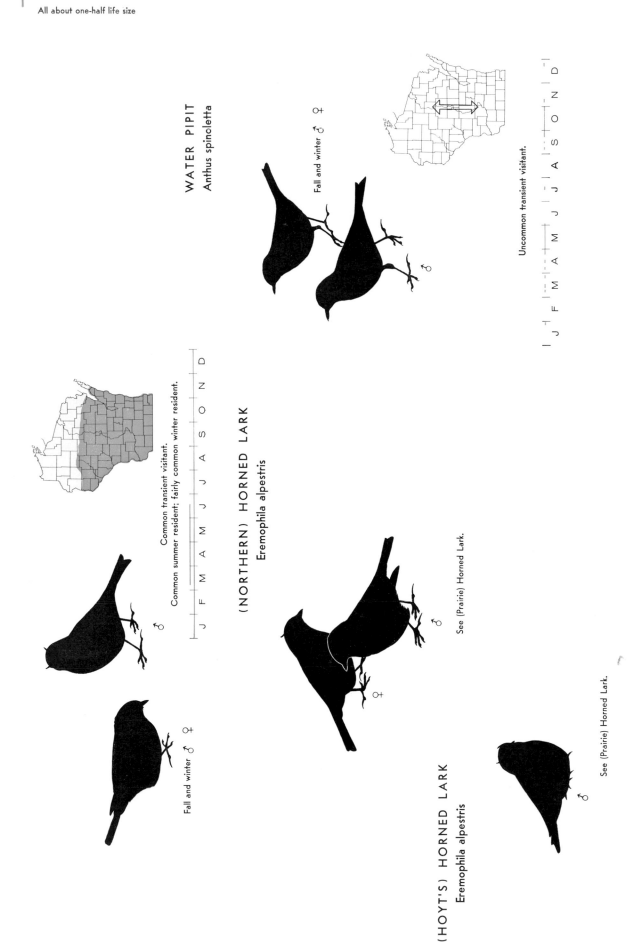

WATER PIPIT
Anthus spinoletta

Fall and winter ♂ ♀

Uncommon transient visitant.

J F M A M J J A S O N D

(PRAIRIE) HORNED LARK
Eremophila alpestris

♂

♀

Fall and winter ♂

Common transient visitant.
Common summer resident; fairly common winter resident.

J F M A M J J A S O N D

(NORTHERN) HORNED LARK
Eremophila alpestris

♂

♀

See (Prairie) Horned Lark.

(HOYT'S) HORNED LARK
Eremophila alpestris

♂

See (Prairie) Horned Lark.

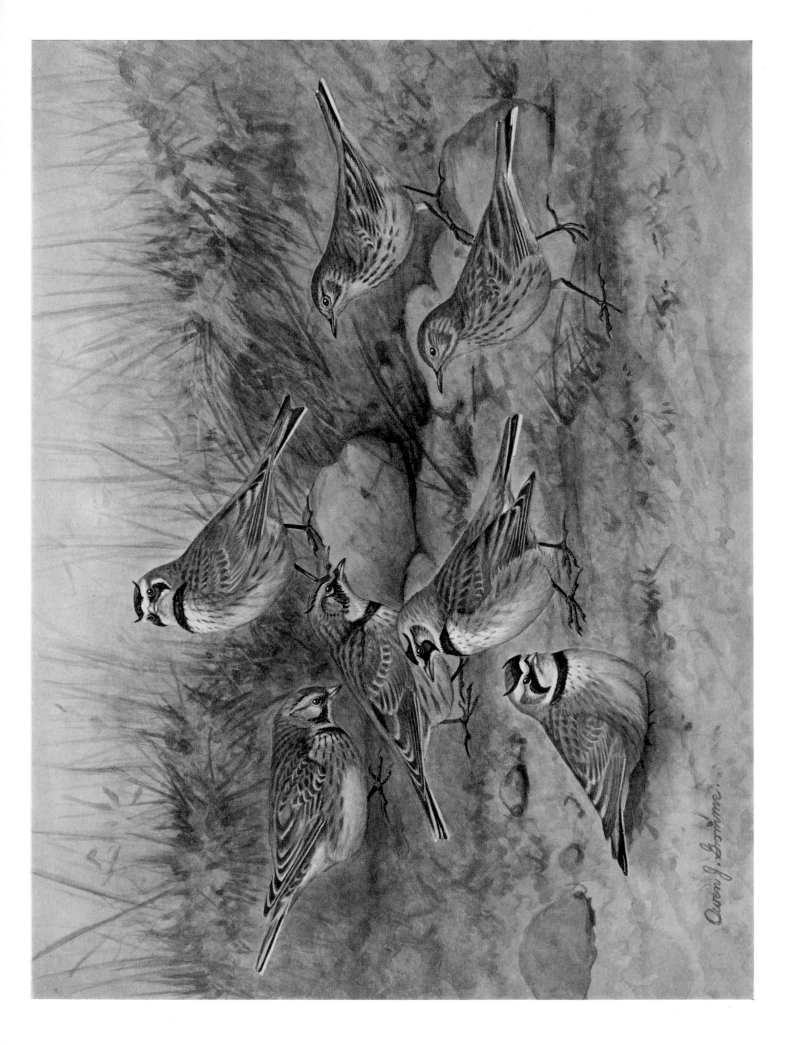

BANK SWALLOW
Riparia riparia

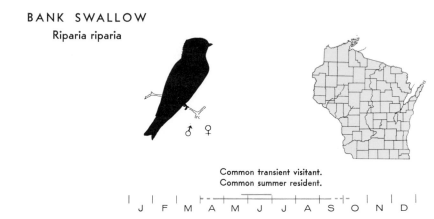

♂ ♀

Common transient visitant.
Common summer resident.

J F M A M J J A S O N D

ROUGH-WINGED SWALLOW
Stelgidopteryx ruficollis

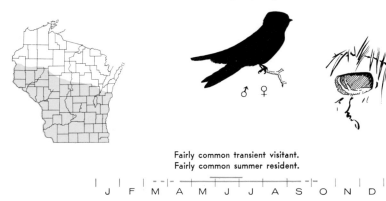

♂ ♀

Fairly common transient visitant.
Fairly common summer resident.

J F M A M J J A S O N D

TREE SWALLOW
Iridoprocne bicolor

♀ ♂

Abundant transient visitant.
Abundant summer resident.

J F M A M J J A S O N D

Plate 55

SWALLOWS and PURPLE MARTIN Family Hirundinidae

About one-half life size

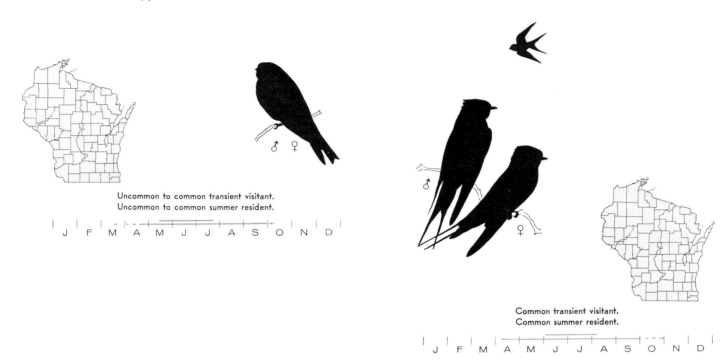

CLIFF SWALLOW
Petrochelidon pyrrhonota

BARN SWALLOW
Hirundo rustica

Uncommon to common transient visitant.
Uncommon to common summer resident.

J F M A M J J A S O N D

Common transient visitant.
Common summer resident.

J F M A M J J A S O N D

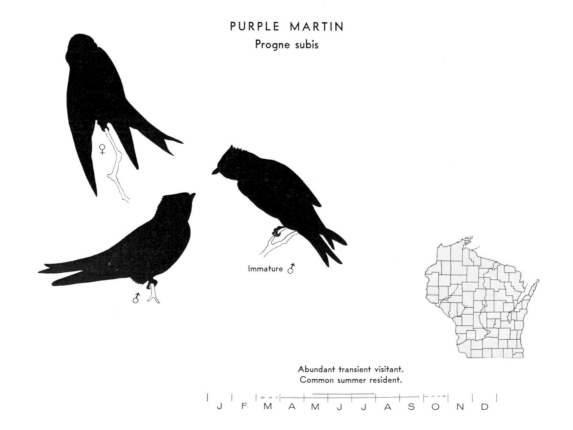

PURPLE MARTIN
Progne subis

Immature ♂

Abundant transient visitant.
Common summer resident.

J F M A M J J A S O N D

111

GRAY JAY
Perisoreus canadensis

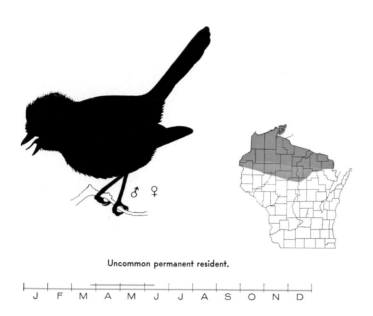

Uncommon permanent resident.

J F M A M J J A S O N D

BLUE JAY
Cyanocitta cristata

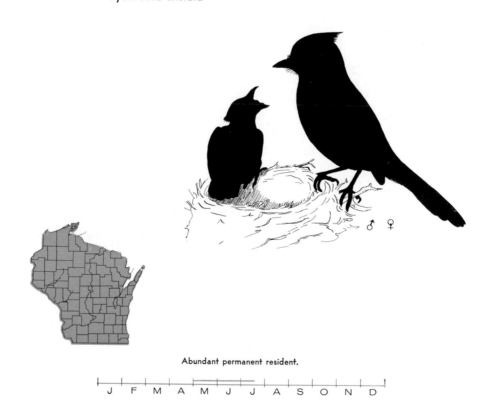

Abundant permanent resident.

J F M A M J J A S O N D

113

BLACK-BILLED MAGPIE
Pica pica

Very rare.

COMMON CROW
Corvus brachyrhynchos

Rare to uncommon winter visitant and abundant summer resident in north.
Abundant permanent resident in south and central.

COMMON RAVEN
Corvus corax

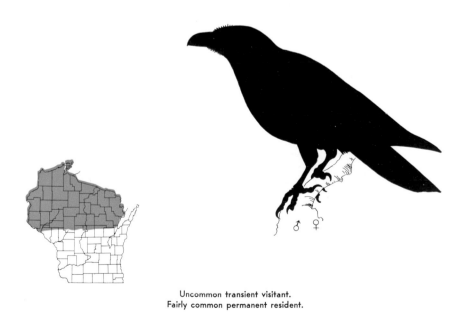

Uncommon transient visitant.
Fairly common permanent resident.

All about one-half life size

TUFTED TITMOUSE
Parus bicolor

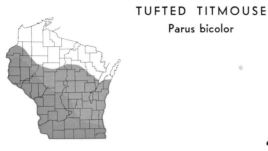

Uncommon permanent resident.

J F M A M J J A S O N D

BROWN CREEPER
Certhia familiaris

Fairly common transient visitant.
Uncommon summer resident; uncommon to fairly common winter resident.

J F M A M J J A S O N D

BOREAL CHICKADEE
Parus hudsonicus

 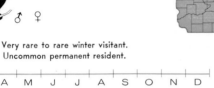

Very rare to rare winter visitant.
Uncommon permanent resident.

J F M A M J J A S O N D

BLACK-CAPPED CHICKADEE
Parus atricapillus

 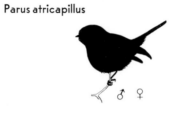

Abundant permanent resident.

J F M A M J J A S O N D

WHITE-BREASTED NUTHATCH
Sitta carolinensis

RED-BREASTED NUTHATCH
Sitta canadensis

Fairly common permanent resident.
Fairly common winter resident.

J F M A M J J A S O N D

Fairly common to common permanent resident.

J F M A M J J A S O N D

Plate 59 | **WRENS** Family Troglodytidae
About one-half life size

BEWICK'S WREN
Thryomanes bewickii

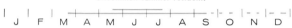

Uncommon transient visitant.
Uncommon summer resident.

HOUSE WREN
Troglodytes aedon

Common transient visitant.
Common summer resident.

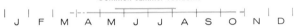

SHORT-BILLED MARSH WREN
Cistothorus platensis

Common transient visitant.
Common summer resident.

CAROLINA WREN
Thryothorus ludovicianus

Rare.

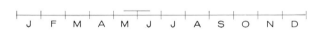

LONG-BILLED MARSH WREN
Telmatodytes palustris

Abundant transient visitant.
Abundant summer resident.

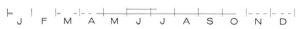

WINTER WREN
Troglodytes troglodytes

Fairly common transient visitant.
Rare to uncommon summer resident; rare winter resident.

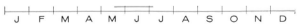

118

119

THRASHER, MOCKINGBIRD, and CATBIRD Family Mimidae

All about one-half life size

TOWNSEND'S SOLITAIRE
Myadestes townsendi

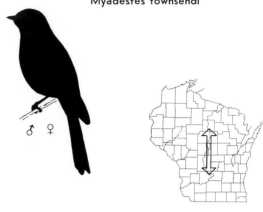

Very rare winter visitant.

J F M A M J J A S O N D

BROWN THRASHER
Toxostoma rufum

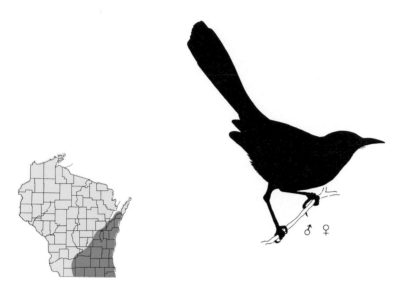

Common transient visitant.
Uncommon to common summer resident; rare winter resident.

J F M A M J J A S O N D

MOCKINGBIRD
Mimus polyglottos

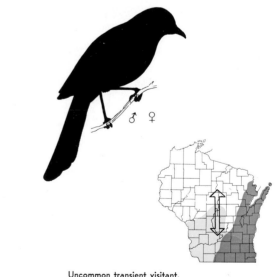

Uncommon transient visitant.
Rare summer resident; uncommon winter resident.

J F M A M J J A S O N D

CATBIRD
Dumetella carolinensis

Common transient visitant.
Common summer resident; very rare winter resident.

J F M A M J J A S O N D

Plate 61 | **THRUSHES** Family Turdidae
About one-half life size

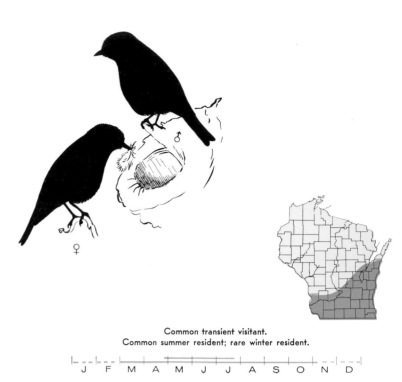

EASTERN BLUEBIRD
Sialia sialis

Common transient visitant.
Common summer resident; rare winter resident.

J F M A M J J A S O N D

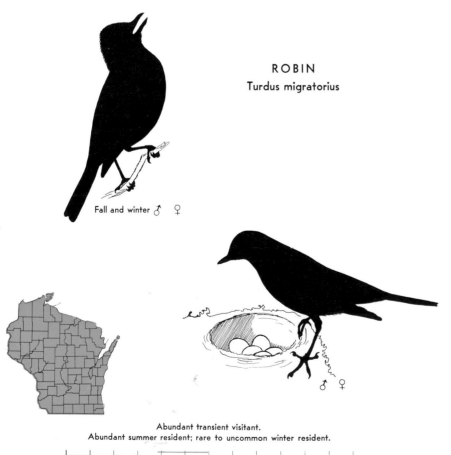

ROBIN
Turdus migratorius

Fall and winter ♂ ♀

Abundant transient visitant.
Abundant summer resident; rare to uncommon winter resident.

J F M A M J J A S O N D

SWAINSON'S THRUSH
Hylocichla ustulata

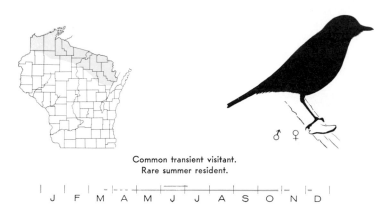

♂ ♀

Common transient visitant.
Rare summer resident.

| J | F | M | A | M | J | J | A | S | O | N | D |

GRAY-CHEEKED THRUSH
Hylocichla minima

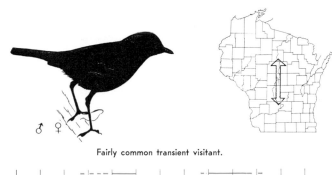

♂ ♀

Fairly common transient visitant.

| J | F | M | A | M | J | J | A | S | O | N | D |

WOOD THRUSH
Hylocichla mustelina

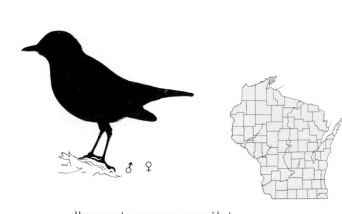

♂ ♀

Uncommon to common summer resident.

| J | F | M | A | M | J | J | A | S | O | N | D |

HERMIT THRUSH
Hylocichla guttata

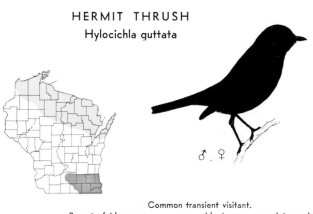

♂ ♀

Common transient visitant.
Rare to fairly common summer resident; very rare winter resident.

| J | F | M | A | M | J | J | A | S | O | N | D |

VEERY
Hylocichla fuscescens

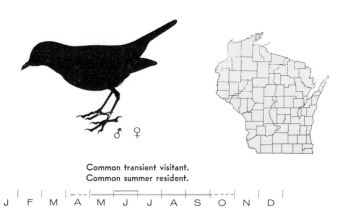

♂ ♀

Common transient visitant.
Common summer resident.

| J | F | M | A | M | J | J | A | S | O | N | D |

125

RUBY-CROWNED KINGLET
Regulus calendula

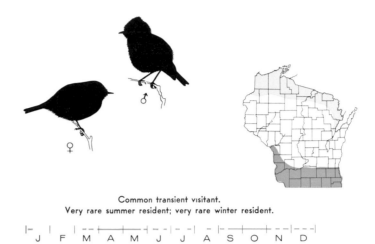

Common transient visitant.
Very rare summer resident; very rare winter resident.

J F M A M J J A S O N D

GOLDEN-CROWNED KINGLET
Regulus satrapa

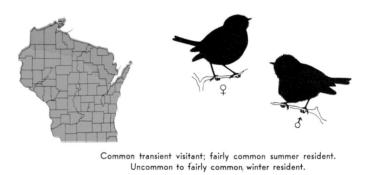

Common transient visitant; fairly common summer resident.
Uncommon to fairly common winter resident.

J F M A M J J A S O N D

BLUE-GRAY GNATCATCHER
Polioptila caerulea

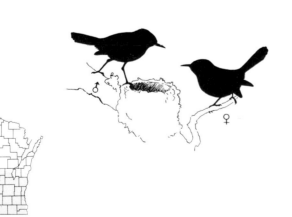

Rare to uncommon summer resident.

J F M A M J J A S O N D

BOHEMIAN WAXWING
Bombycilla garrulus

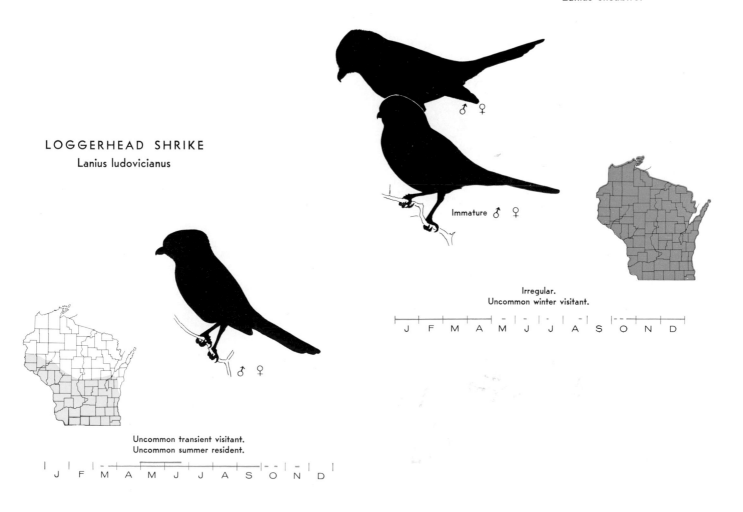

Irregular
Uncommon winter visitant.

J F M A M J J A S O N D

CEDAR WAXWING
Bombycilla cedrorum

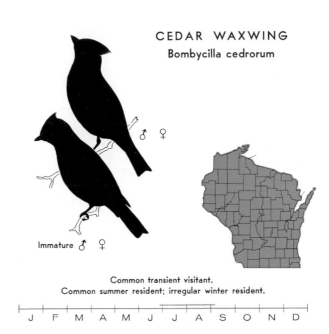

Immature ♂ ♀

Common transient visitant.
Common summer resident; irregular winter resident.

J F M A M J J A S O N D

NORTHERN SHRIKE
Lanius excubitor

Immature ♂ ♀

Irregular.
Uncommon winter visitant.

J F M A M J J A S O N D

LOGGERHEAD SHRIKE
Lanius ludovicianus

♂ ♀

Uncommon transient visitant.
Uncommon summer resident.

J F M A M J J A S O N D

Plate 65 | VIREOS Family Vireonidae

About one-half life size

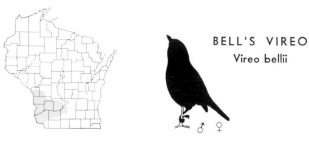

BELL'S VIREO
Vireo bellii

Rare summer resident locally.

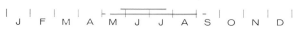

WHITE-EYED VIREO
Vireo griseus

Rare transient visitant in south.
Rare summer resident in south.

RED-EYED VIREO
Vireo olivaceus

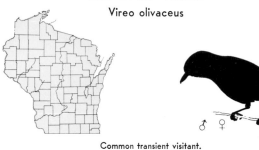

Common transient visitant.
Common summer resident.

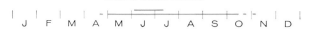

WARBLING VIREO
Vireo gilvus

Common transient visitant.
Common summer resident.

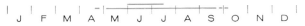

SOLITARY VIREO
Vireo solitarius

Fairly common transient visitant.
Fairly common summer resident.

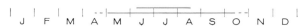

YELLOW-THROATED VIREO
Vireo flavifrons

Fairly common transient visitant.
Fairly common summer resident.

PHILADELPHIA VIREO
Vireo philadelphicus

Uncommon transient visitant.

TENNESSEE WARBLER
Vermivora peregrina

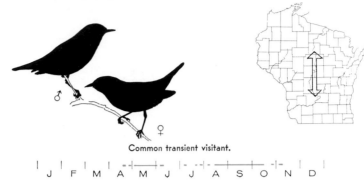

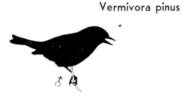

Common transient visitant.

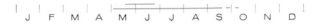

J F M A M J J A S O N D

BLUE-WINGED WARBLER
Vermivora pinus

Uncommon to fairly common summer resident.

J F M A M J J A S O N D

BLACK-AND-WHITE WARBLER
Mniotilta varia

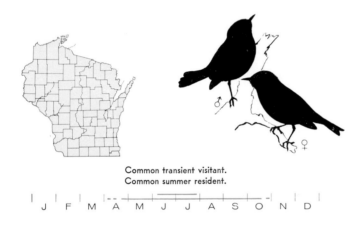

Common transient visitant.
Common summer resident.

J F M A M J J A S O N D

GOLDEN-WINGED WARBLER
Vermivora chrysoptera

Fairly common summer resident.

J F M A M J J A S O N D

PROTHONOTARY WARBLER
Protonotaria citrea

Uncommon transient visitant.
Uncommon to rare summer resident.

J F M A M J J A S O N D

WORM-EATING WARBLER
Helmitheros vermivorus

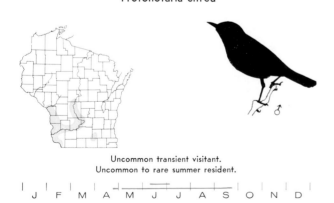

Very rare transient visitant in south.

J F M A M J J A S O N D

Plate 67 | WOOD WARBLERS Family Parulidae
About one-half life size

PARULA WARBLER
Parula americana

Fairly common transient visitant.
Fairly common summer resident.

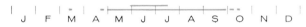
J F M A M J J A S O N D

ORANGE-CROWNED WARBLER
Vermivora celata

Uncommon transient visitant.

J F M A M J J A S O N D

YELLOW WARBLER
Dendroica petechia

Common transient visitant.
Common summer resident.

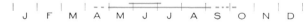
J F M A M J J A S O N D

NASHVILLE WARBLER
Vermivora ruficapilla

Fairly common transient visitant.
Rare to fairly common summer resident.

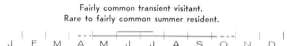
J F M A M J J A S O N D

134

CAPE MAY WARBLER
Dendroica tigrina

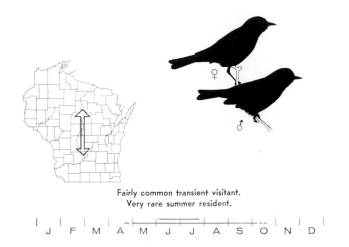

Fairly common transient visitant.
Very rare summer resident.

J F M A M J J A S O N D

MAGNOLIA WARBLER
Dendroica magnolia

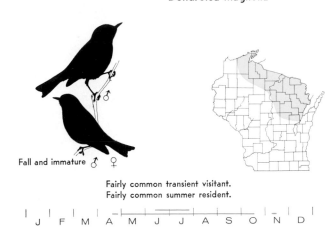

Fall and immature ♂ ♀

Fairly common transient visitant.
Fairly common summer resident.

J F M A M J J A S O N D

MYRTLE WARBLER
Dendroica coronata

Fall and immature ♂ ♀

Abundant transient visitant.
Uncommon summer resident; very rare winter resident.

J F M A M J J A S O N D

BLACK-THROATED GREEN WARBLER
Dendroica virens

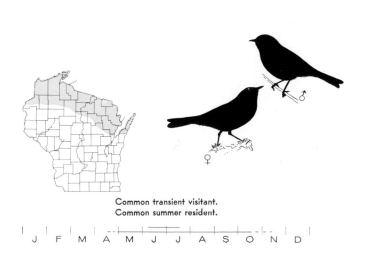

Common transient visitant.
Common summer resident.

J F M A M J J A S O N D

BLACK-THROATED BLUE WARBLER
Dendroica caerulescens

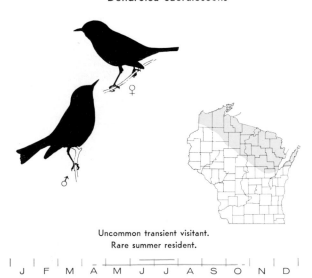

Uncommon transient visitant.
Rare summer resident.

J F M A M J J A S O N D

137

Plate 69 | **WOOD WARBLERS** Family Parulidae
About one-half life size

BAY-BREASTED WARBLER
Dendroica castanea

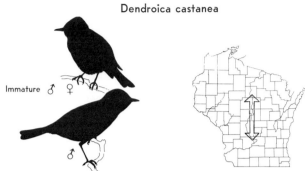

Immature ♂ ♀

♂

Fairly common transient visitant.

J F M A M J J A S O N D

BLACKPOLL WARBLER
Dendroica striata

♀

Fairly common transient visitant.

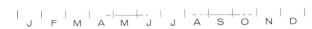

J F M A M J J A S O N D

YELLOW-THROATED WARBLER
Dendroica dominica

♂

Very rare.

J F M A M J J A S O N D

BLACKBURNIAN WARBLER
Dendroica fusca

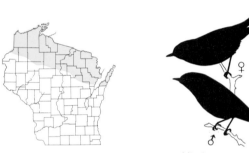

♀

♂

Common transient visitant.
Fairly common summer resident.

J F M A M J J A S O N D

CERULEAN WARBLER
Dendroica cerulea

♂

♀

Uncommon summer resident.

J F M A M J J A S O N D

CHESTNUT-SIDED WARBLER
Dendroica pensylvanica

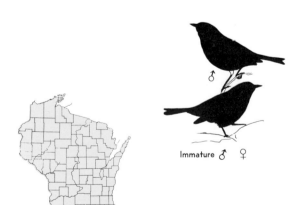

♂

Immature ♂ ♀

Common transient visitant.
Fairly common to common summer resident.

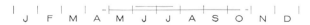

J F M A M J J A S O N D

PINE WARBLER
Dendroica pinus

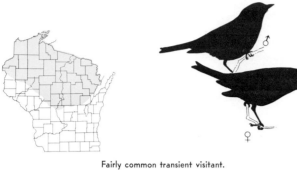

Fairly common transient visitant.
Fairly common summer resident locally.

J F M A M J J A S O N D

PRAIRIE WARBLER
Dendroica discolor

Rare.

J F M A M J J A S O N D

PALM WARBLER
Dendroica palmarum

Common transient visitant.
Rare summer resident.

J F M A M J J A S O N D

NORTHERN WATERTHRUSH
Seiurus noveboracensis

Fairly common transient visitant.
Uncommon summer resident.

J F M A M J J A S O N D

OVENBIRD
Seiurus aurocapillus

Abundant transient visitant.
Common summer resident.

J F M A M J J A S O N D

LOUISIANA WATERTHRUSH
Seiurus motacilla

Uncommon transient visitant in south and east.
Uncommon summer resident.

J F M A M J J A S O N D

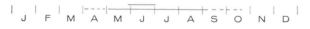

Plate 71 | **WOOD WARBLERS** Family Parulidae

About one-half life size

KENTUCKY WARBLER
Oporornis formosus

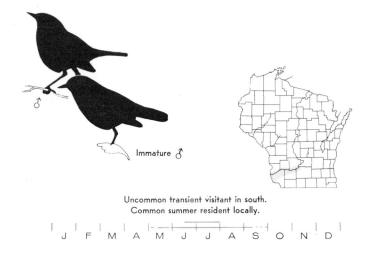

Immature ♂

Uncommon transient visitant in south.
Common summer resident locally.

J F M A M J J A S O N D

YELLOW-BREASTED CHAT
Icteria virens

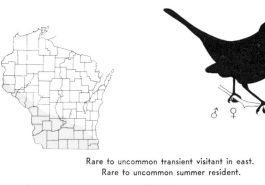

♂ ♀

Rare to uncommon transient visitant in east.
Rare to uncommon summer resident.

J F M A M J J A S O N D

MOURNING WARBLER
Oporornis philadelphia

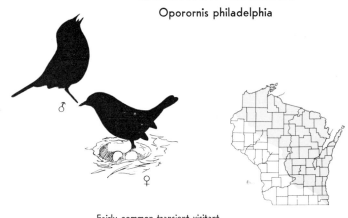

♂

♀

Fairly common transient visitant.
Fairly common summer resident.

J F M A M J J A S O N D

YELLOWTHROAT
Geothlypis trichas

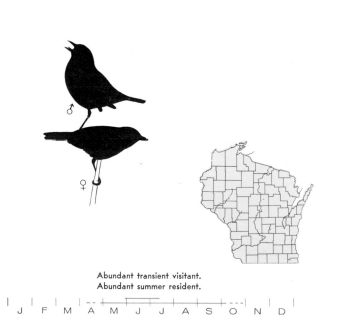

♂

♀

Abundant transient visitant.
Abundant summer resident.

J F M A M J J A S O N D

CONNECTICUT WARBLER
Oporornis agilis

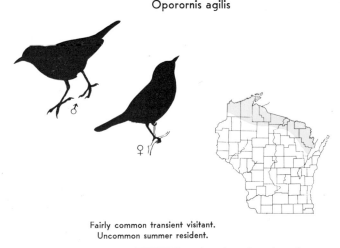

♂

♀

Fairly common transient visitant.
Uncommon summer resident.

J F M A M J J A S O N D

142

AMERICAN REDSTART
Setophaga ruticilla

Immature ♂

Abundant transient visitant.
Common summer resident.

J F M A M J J A S O N D

HOODED WARBLER
Wilsonia citrina

Rare transient visitant in south.

J F M A M J J A S O N D

WILSON'S WARBLER
Wilsonia pusilla

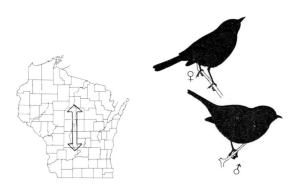

Fairly common transient visitant.

J F M A M J J A S O N D

CANADA WARBLER
Wilsonia canadensis

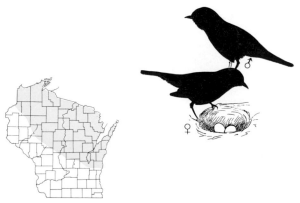

Common transient visitant.
Fairly common summer resident.

J F M A M J J A S O N D

EVENING GROSBEAK
Hesperiphona vespertina

Fairly common transient visitant.
Rare summer resident; fairly common winter resident.

HOUSE SPARROW
Passer domesticus

Abundant permanent resident.

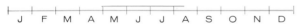

DICKCISSEL
Spiza americana

Uncommon to fairly common transient visitant irregularly.
Uncommon to fairly common summer resident irregularly.

PINE GROSBEAK
Pinicola enucleator

Uncommon to fairly common winter visitant.

More Grosbeaks on plates 80 and 83

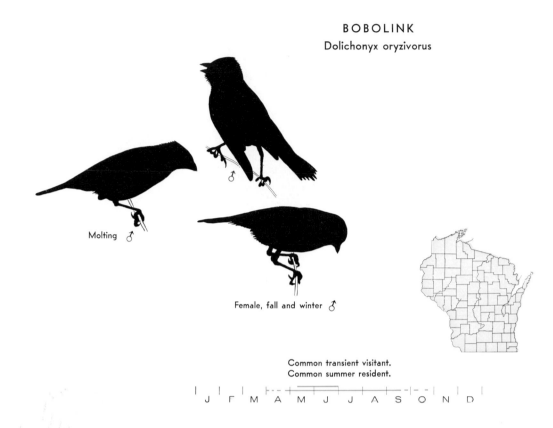

BOBOLINK
Dolichonyx oryzivorus

Molting ♂

Female, fall and winter ♂

Common transient visitant.
Common summer resident.

J F M A M J J A S O N D

WESTERN MEADOWLARK
Sturnella neglecta

EASTERN MEADOWLARK
Sturnella magna

Common transient visitant.
Common to uncommon summer resident; uncommon winter resident.

J F M A M J J A S O N D

Abundant transient visitant.
Abundant summer resident; uncommon winter resident.

J F M A M J J A S O N D

149

Plate 75 | BLACKBIRDS Family Icteridae

About one-half life size

YELLOW-HEADED BLACKBIRD

Xanthocephalus xanthocephalus

Fairly common summer resident locally.

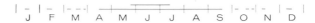

REDWINGED BLACKBIRD

Agelaius phoeniceus

Immature ♂

Abundant transient visitant; abundant summer resident.
Uncommon to locally abundant winter resident.

ORCHARD ORIOLE
Icterus spurius

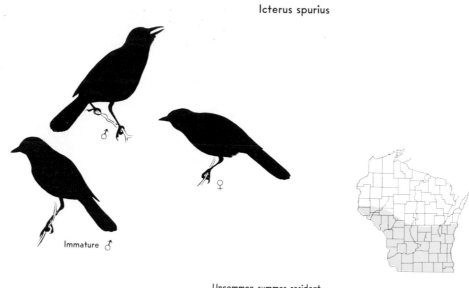

Immature ♂

♂

♀

Uncommon summer resident.

J F M A M J J A S O N D

BALTIMORE ORIOLE
Icterus galbula

Immature ♂

♀

♂

Common transient visitant.
Common summer resident.

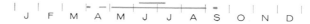

J F M A M J J A S O N D

Plate 77 | **BLACKBIRDS** Family Icteridae
About one-half life size

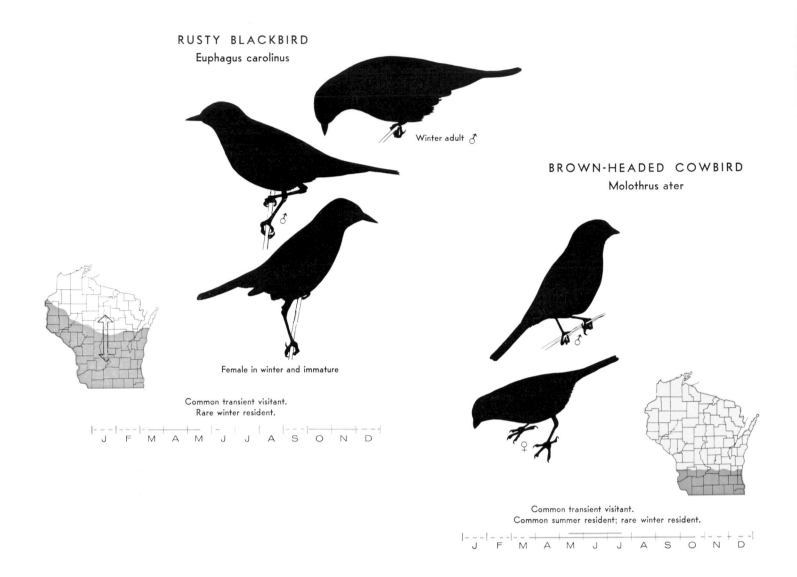

RUSTY BLACKBIRD
Euphagus carolinus

Winter adult ♂

Female in winter and immature

Common transient visitant.
Rare winter resident.

J F M A M J J A S O N D

BROWN-HEADED COWBIRD
Molothrus ater

Common transient visitant.
Common summer resident; rare winter resident.

J F M A M J J A S O N D

BREWER'S BLACKBIRD
Euphagus cyanocephalus

♂   ♀

Fairly common transient visitant.
Fairly common summer resident; very rare winter resident.

J F M A M J J A S O N D

STARLING
Sturnus vulgaris

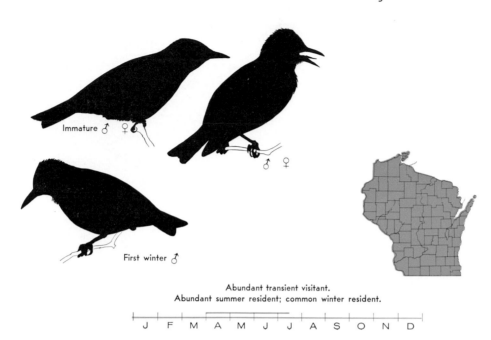

Immature ♂ ♀

First winter ♂

Abundant transient visitant.
Abundant summer resident; common winter resident.

J F M A M J J A S O N D

COMMON GRACKLE
Quiscalus quiscula

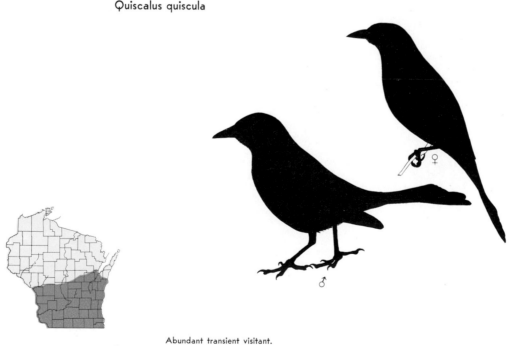

♀

♂

Abundant transient visitant.
Common summer resident; uncommon winter resident.

J F M A M J J A S O N D

Plate 79 | **TANAGERS** Family Thraupidae

About one-half life size

SUMMER TANAGER
Piranga rubra

♀

WESTERN TANAGER
Piranga ludoviciana

Very rare.

J F M A M J J A S O N D

♂

Accidental.

J F M A M J J A S O N D

SCARLET TANAGER
Piranga olivacea

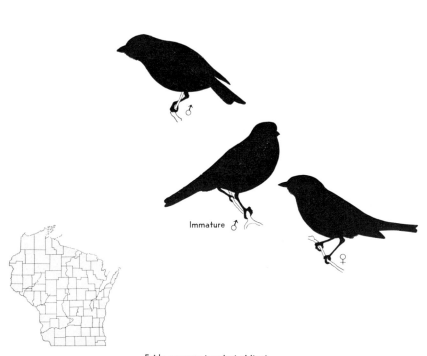

♂

Immature ♂

♀

Fairly common transient visitant.
Fairly common summer resident.

J F M A M J J A S O N D

ROSE-BREASTED GROSBEAK
Pheucticus ludovicianus

Immature ♂

♀

♂

Common transient visitant.
Common summer resident.

J F M A M J J A S O N D

CARDINAL
Richmondena cardinalis

♂

♀

Common permanent resident.

J F M A M J J A S O N D

RUFOUS-SIDED TOWHEE
Pipilo erythrophthalmus

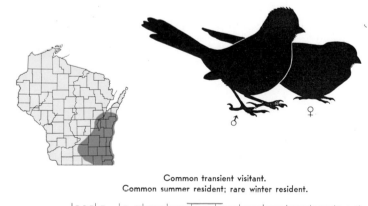

♂ ♀

Common transient visitant.
Common summer resident; rare winter resident.

J F M A M J J A S O N D

INDIGO BUNTING
Passerina cyanea

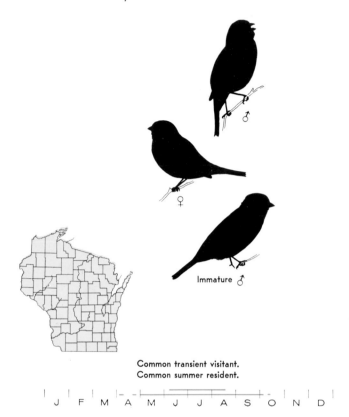

Immature ♂

Common transient visitant.
Common summer resident.

J F M A M J J A S O N D

PINE SISKIN
Spinus pinus

♀

Uncommon transient visitant.
Rare summer resident; uncommon winter resident.

J F M A M J J A S O N D

AMERICAN GOLDFINCH
Spinus tristis

Winter ♂   ♀

♀   ♂

Abundant transient visitant.
Common summer resident; uncommon to common winter resident.

J F M A M J J A S O N D

About one-half life size

COMMON REDPOLL
Acanthis flammea

Common but irregular winter visitant.

J F M A M J J A S O N D

HOARY REDPOLL
Acanthis hornemanni

Rare to uncommon winter visitant.

J F M A M J J A S O N D

(HOLBOELL'S) COMMON REDPOLL
Acanthis flammea

See Common Redpoll.

(GREATER) COMMON REDPOLL
Acanthis flammea

See Common Redpoll.

PURPLE FINCH
Carpodacus purpureus

Female, immature ♂

Fairly common transient visitant.
Fairly common summer resident; fairly common winter resident.

J F M A M J J A S O N D

WHITE-WINGED CROSSBILL
Loxia leucoptera

Immature ♂

Uncommon and irregular winter visitant.
Rare summer resident.

J F M A M J J A S O N D

RED CROSSBILL
Loxia curvirostra

Rare summer resident.
Irregular winter resident.

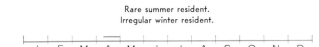
J F M A M J J A S O N D

BLUE GROSBEAK
Guiraca caerulea

Very rare transient visitant in south.

J F M A M J J A S O N D

166

LARK SPARROW
Chondestes grammacus

Uncommon summer resident.

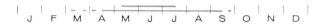

VESPER SPARROW
Pooecetes gramineus

Common transient visitant.
Common summer resident; rare to very rare winter resident.

SHARP-TAILED SPARROW
Ammospiza caudacuta

Rare transient visitant.

HENSLOW'S SPARROW
Passerherbulus henslowii

Fairly common summer resident.

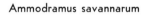

LE CONTE'S SPARROW
Passerherbulus caudacutus

Rare transient visitant.
Rare summer resident.

GRASSHOPPER SPARROW
Ammodramus savannarum

Fairly common summer resident locally.

SAVANNAH SPARROW
Passerculus sandwichensis

Common transient visitant.
Common summer resident.

CHIPPING SPARROW
Spizella passerina

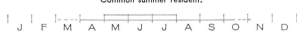

Common transient visitant.
Common summer resident.

J F M A M J J A S O N D

TREE SPARROW
Spizella arborea

Abundant transient visitant.
Rare to common winter resident.

J F M A M J J A S O N D

CLAY-COLORED SPARROW
Spizella pallida

Fairly common transient visitant.
Fairly common summer resident locally.

J F M A M J J A S O N D

(MONTANA) OREGON JUNCO
Junco oreganus

Rare winter resident.

J F M A M J J A S O N D

SLATE-COLORED JUNCO
Junco hyemalis

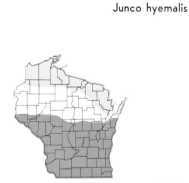

Abundant transient visitant.
Uncommon summer resident; common winter resident.

J F M A M J J A S O N D

FIELD SPARROW
Spizella pusilla

Common transient visitant.
Common summer resident; rare winter resident.

J F M A M J J A S O N D

170

Owen J. Gromme.

HARRIS' SPARROW
Zonotrichia querula

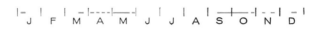

Immature ♂ ♀

Uncommon transient visitant.

J F M A M J J A S O N D

GOLDEN-CROWNED SPARROW
Zonotrichia atricapilla

Accidental.

(GAMBEL'S) WHITE-CROWNED SPARROW
Zonotrichia leucophrys

♂ ♀

See White-crowned Sparrow.

WHITE-CROWNED SPARROW
Zonotrichia leucophrys

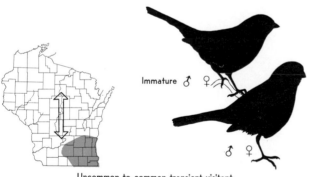

Immature ♂ ♀

Uncommon to common transient visitant.
Very rare winter resident.

J F M A M J J A S O N D

WHITE-THROATED SPARROW
Zonotrichia albicollis

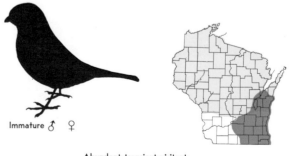

Immature ♂ ♀

Abundant transient visitant.
Rare to common summer resident; rare winter resident.

J F M A M J J A S O N D

Plate 87 | SPARROWS Family Fringillidae
About one-half life size

FOX SPARROW
Passerella iliaca

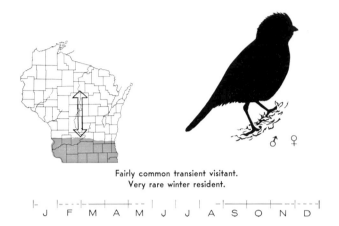

Fairly common transient visitant.
Very rare winter resident.

J F M A M J J A S O N D

SONG SPARROW
Melospiza melodia

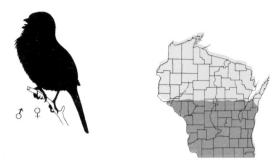

Abundant transient visitant.
Abundant summer resident; uncommon winter resident.

J F M A M J J A S O N D

SWAMP SPARROW
Melospiza georgiana

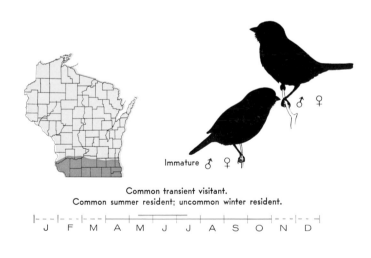

Immature ♂ ♀

Common transient visitant.
Common summer resident; uncommon winter resident.

J F M A M J J A S O N D

LINCOLN'S SPARROW
Melospiza lincolnii

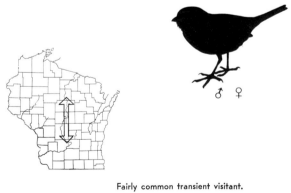

♂ ♀

Fairly common transient visitant.

J F M A M J J A S O N D

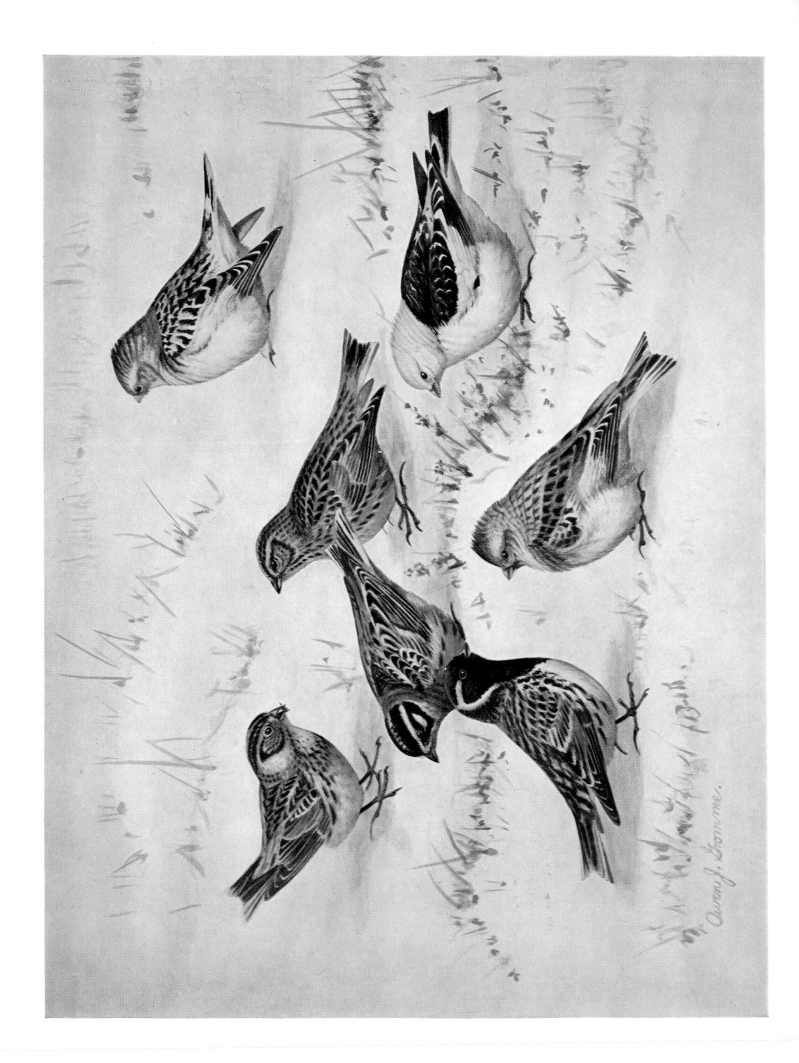

Owen J. Gromme.

SNOW BUNTING
Plectrophenax nivalis

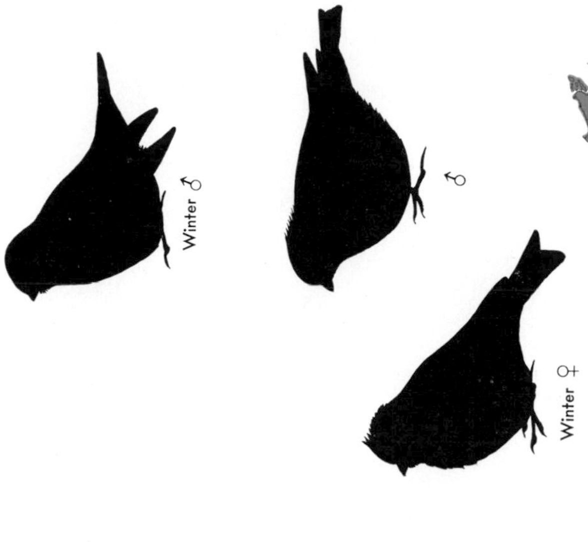

Winter ♂

♂

Winter ♀

Uncommon to common transient visitant.
Uncommon to common winter resident.

J F M A M J J A S O N D

SMITH'S LONGSPUR
Calcarius pictus

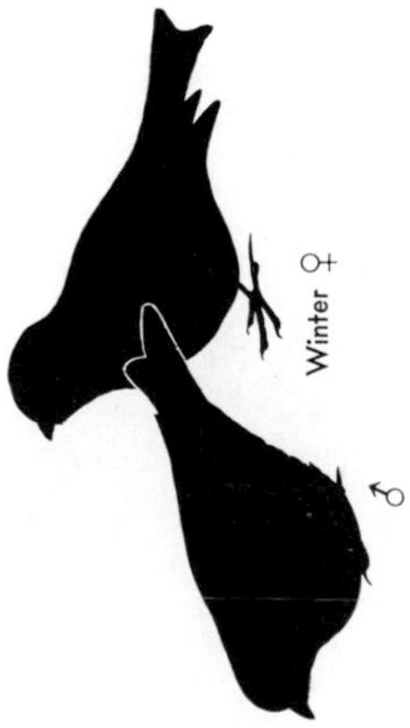

Winter ♀

♂

Accidental.

J F M A M J J A S O N D

LAPLAND LONGSPUR
Calcarius lapponicus

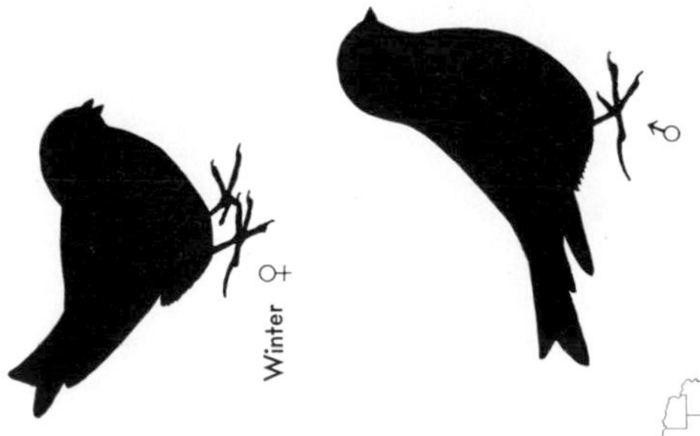

Winter ♀

♂

Common transient visitant.
Uncommon to common winter resident.

J F M A M J J A S O N D

Plate 89 | H E R O N and E G R E T Family Ardeidae

G A L L I N U L E Family Rallidae and O W L Family Strigidae

All about one-fourth life size

LITTLE BLUE HERON
Florida caerulea

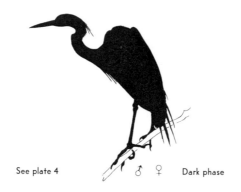

See plate 4   ♂ ♀   Dark phase

BURROWING OWL
Speotyto cunicularia

♂ ♀

Very rare transient visitant.

J F M A M J J A S O N D

CATTLE EGRET
Bubulcus ibis

♂ ♀

Very rare transient visitant.

J F M A M J J A S O N D

PURPLE GALLINULE
Porphyrula martinica

♂ ♀

Accidental.

BIRDS IN ACTION AND IN HABITAT

For its size and weight, the Goshawk is probably the strongest and most savage of American birds of prey. Because its customary habitat is the forests of the far north where it has little contact with man, it has no fear of hunters and falls easy prey to them. This hawk has been known to attack a man without hesitation, a fact which I can personally confirm.

The Goshawk's uncommon and irregular visits to Wisconsin usually occur during hard winters when it is driven south in search of food, and the bird rarely nests here. A Goshawk had never been photographed at its nest before 1934, when a pair of nesting birds was reported in Rusk County. I was a member of the party which succeeded in procuring the first photographs, and in 1936 I painted this study from prints of those negatives.

Accipiter gentilis (Plate 15). Oil (24″ by 30″) owned by the author.

The familiar feud between owls and crows is portrayed in this study of a Great Horned Owl and its assailants. Powerful and well armed though it may be, many a battered and befuddled owl has been temporarily bested by these persistent tormentors, until nightfall reverses the advantage. Hunters using a mechanical or mounted owl as a decoy take advantage of this natural enmity to lure crows which cannot resist the opportunity of a daylight attack on an owl out in the open. Sometimes hundreds of crows are shot in a few hours by the use of such a decoy.

Bubo virginianus (Plate 44). *Corvus brachyrhynchos* (Plate 57). Oil (24″ by 30″) painted in 1956 and owned by Mr. Hermann A. Nunnemacher, of Pewaukee, Wisconsin.

The Peregrine Falcon, in this country long known as the Duck Hawk, was formerly a familiar sight in Wisconsin as a migrant or summer resident. In recent years its numbers have so decreased because of the persistent robbing of its nests by egg collectors and by persons wishing to revive the ancient sport of falconry that state laws now protect the bird. This painting, inspired by a scene I witnessed near Fond du Lac, shows an immature male plummeting at a pair of Green-winged Teal in the steep dive for which the falcon is noted. The bird I saw and painted in 1937 was apparently either practicing a dive or teasing the teal, for it did not complete the attack.

Falco peregrinus (Plate 19). *Anas carolinensis* (Plate 8). Oil (24″ by 30″) owned by the author.

The Ruffed Grouse is for many the undisputed king of our upland game birds. It is nonmigratory and can survive in the cool shade of heavy brush during the hottest summers and in heavy cover during severe winters. In late fall it grows "snowshoes," or serrations on the sides of each toe, which help give it support on the surface of deep snow. Predators such as the Goshawk and the Snowy Owl attack it during the winter, when snow on the ground makes it particularly conspicuous.

The gradually accelerated drumming sound produced when the bird beats the air with its wings was in former years a commonplace accompaniment of spring in all of our more extensive wooded areas, and is still familiar in all of Wisconsin except for areas of intensive agriculture in the southeast. This mating sound can be heard throughout the year, though as the seasons advance it becomes less and less frequent. The bird's name comes from the ruff displayed conspicuously by the male when it drums, or spreads its tail feathers while strutting in the presence of females.

Bonasa umbellus (Plate 21). Oil (30″ by 40″) painted in 1961 and owned by Mr. Harold P. Mueller, Sr., of Delray Beach, Florida.

The cheery call of the Bobwhite, another fine game bird, is a familiar and welcome sound to farmers over large areas of the United States. Intensive management, particularly in the southern states, has made quail hunting a popular sport. Central Wisconsin is the northern limit of the bird's range, and severe winters can wipe out the population over large areas. The typically large broods of young each spring usually compensate rapidly for the annual winter loss. Where roadsides adjacent to farming areas provide winter cover and suitable nesting, the species thrives. This painting was made near Briggsville, Wisconsin, in 1958.

Colinus virginianus (Plate 23). Oil (16″ by 20″) owned by Mrs. Parker Poe, of Pebble Hill Plantation, Thomasville, Georgia.

191

Almost every winter a few Snowy Owls wander south from the Arctic tundras in search of food—rodents and other mammals and birds. In snowless winters the predominantly white plumage of the Snowy Owl is conspicuous, an easy mark for a hunter; and in former years hunters shot many of these birds. Now they are protected by law. Here an owl devouring a Ring-necked Pheasant is being harassed by a crow, which is calling its clan to challenge the owl.

Nyctea scandiaca (Plate 44). *Phasianus colchicus* (Plate 23). *Corvus brachyrhynchos* (Plate 57). Water color (16″ by 21″) painted in 1953 and owned by Dr. Alfred Wallner, of Kalispel, Montana.

Once considered a prized addition to the menu of any fine restaurant, Canvasback were shipped to city markets by the barrelful. Restrictions on hunting have only partially retarded the rapid decline of this once abundant species. The drainage of its breeding grounds in the prairies (United States and Canada) continues to restrict growth of the population.

In October and November great flocks of Canvasback used to be a familiar sight along the shallow west shore of Lake Winnebago, on the larger lakes of the Fox River valley, and especially on Lake Koshkonong. The picture opposite recalls a wet and foggy fall day on Lake Winnebago in 1957 when Canvasback were still with us in numbers. This flock of birds hesitated in flight for a brief moment to satisfy their curiosity about hunters' decoys before fading rapidly away into the mist, unaware of their close call.

Aythya valisineria (Plate 10). Oil (24″ by 36″) painted in 1958 and owned by Mr. Frederick L. Ott, of Milwaukee, Wisconsin.

The hardy Ruffed Grouse, a familiar permanent resident in Wisconsin, often uses snow as protection against predators and the cold of winter. On nights when it does not roost among the protecting limbs of conifers, the grouse will sometimes remain quiet on the older crust of the snow and allow new snowfall to bury it to a depth of several inches, or it may plunge headlong into soft snow to spend the night. If an intruder steps too close, the Ruffed Grouse erupts from its hiding place with explosive suddenness amid a geyser of snow as it escapes toward the nearest heavy cover. In this picture a weasel, or ermine, on its daily prowl for food meets with a sudden surprise.

Bonasa umbellus (Plate 21). Water color (18″ by 24″) painted in 1953 and owned by Mr. and Mrs. Frank Howard, of Woodstock, Illinois.

Most Sandhill Cranes pass beyond Wisconsin borders and spend their summers in the far north, but a few remain with us and nest on the larger and less accessible marshlands and bogs of the state. The Sandhill Game Farm in central Wisconsin, once a vast wasteland of drained marshes and abandoned farms, has become famous as a gathering place of this strikingly graceful species. This picture of a flock of tired Sandhills coming in for a landing against a strong buffeting wind was painted there one crisp October morning in 1958. I will never forget the sound of penetrating trumpeting as they announced their arrival.

Grus canadensis (Plate 25). Oil (24″ by 36″) owned by the author.

The Mallard is the original wild stock from which most of the domestic ducks of the world originated, and is widely distributed throughout the northern hemisphere. Its savory flesh and large size make it a favorite table bird and a particular prize of sportsmen wherever it is found, just as its beauty of color, tolerance of man, and the readiness with which it breeds in captivity or semi-domesticity make it a familiar ornamental waterfowl.

Equally at home in a variety of habitats, the Mallard once frequented the wild-rice beds of Wisconsin in great numbers during spring and fall migration. With the increasing scarcity of wild rice, it has readily adapted itself to gleaning fields harvested by wasteful corn pickers, so that some Mallard hunting is now done on dry land. The Mallard remains in Wisconsin throughout the winter wherever it can find open water and a supply of food. Around city water areas, where it is fed and protected, it is often a familiar resident. Here is a painting of a small flock, on a cold bright winter day, dropping in to rest on the partly ice-free waters of Cedar Creek in Washington County.

Anas platyrhynchos (Plate 7). Oil (24″ by 30″) painted in 1955 and owned by Mr. Roy O. Gromme, of Milwaukee, Wisconsin.

The timely establishment of large waterfowl refuges along the major flyways of the continent has brought about changes in the habits of wildlife which in turn have created serious problems in game management. Birds must be protected from careless and irresponsible shooting. Predators, such as foxes, thrive in refuges where they find freedom of movement and a ready supply of dead and wounded birds. Here a faithful and protesting gander attendant upon its wounded mate is surprised by a marauding red fox. This painting of Canada Geese was made at Horicon Marsh in the fall of 1959.

Branta canadensis (Plate 6). Oil (24″ by 30″) owned by the author.

203

In many respects the Sharp-tailed Grouse resembles its near relative, the Greater Prairie Chicken; and the general similarity of their habits accounts for the fact that over much of their range the name "chicken" is applied to both. The accompanying picture of a covey of Sharptails landing in an alfalfa field in northern Wisconsin illustrates a good combination of marginal habitat suitable for the continued survival of this diminishing species. The Sharptail is a bird of the bush, especially brushy clearings, but the true Prairie Chicken prefers the open grasslands. Where prairie and brushland meet, the Sharptails and Prairie Chickens often share the same feeding and dancing ground. Both species are rapidly decreasing in number and can be found only in suitable areas in northern and central Wisconsin. When a low second growth covered central Wisconsin after the great fires of the 1920's, conditions were ideal for Sharptails and hunters came to the area from all over the Middle West.

Pedioecetes phasianellus (Plate 22). Oil (26″ by 33″) painted in 1953 and owned by Mr. Arthur Mac-Arthur, of Janesville, Wisconsin.

By the middle of October the flocks of Canada Geese assembled in Wisconsin usually number into the tens of thousands. Chiefly land feeders, the birds remain here as long as food is available or until severe weather drives them south. Harrying of the flocks by hunters up and down the great continental flyways has led to the establishment of large refuges to provide feeding and resting grounds, such as the one at Horicon Marsh where this picture was painted in 1960. Here a flock breaks formation for a long gliding descent to a snow-covered field of picked corn on a cold fall day.

Branta canadensis (Plate 6). Oil (30″ by 40″) owned by Mr. Arthur MacArthur, of Janesville, Wisconsin.

The Greater Prairie Chicken is a true bird of the open grasslands and has moved further and further north in the Middle West as the clearing of the forests for agriculture provided the open country to which it was accustomed elsewhere. Coveys of Prairie Chickens followed the movement of the pioneers for whom they provided an excellent and convenient source of meat. They have declined with increasing human population and intensified agriculture. The State of Wisconsin and dedicated private organizations have been acquiring suitable tracts of land as refuges for this species. It is hoped that through careful management and through the acquisition of more refuge areas the Greater Prairie Chicken can be saved from extinction.

This plate is dedicated to the Society of *Tympanuchus Cupido Pinnatus*, Ltd., for the preservation of this species.

Tympanuchus cupido (Plate 22). Oil (24" by 36") painted in 1957 and owned by the author.

In Wisconsin the spring arrival of migrating swans leads many nature lovers to places where the swans regularly gather, such as Green Bay and the larger lakes of the Fox River valley. No longer legal game for hunters, swans are slowly increasing in numbers. By the first of April thousands of them are usually on the open waters of their favored lakes and the larger rivers in Wisconsin. They stay only briefly before heading to their nesting lakes on the tundra of the far north. The picture of Whistling Swans on the opposite page was painted in 1952, from the memory of swans I saw early one April morning while on a camping trip at a favorite spot in Sheboygan County among the dunes on the shores of Lake Michigan.

Olor columbianus (Plate 6). Oil (28″ by 40″) owned by the author.

The American Woodcock, familiarly known as the "Timber Doodle," arrives in Wisconsin from the south in March, as soon as the ground surface is free of frost, and remains until cold fall weather cuts off its main food supply of worms. Its nearly perfect camouflage and the explosive suddenness of its movements have made the woodcock a challenging target for hunters, producing a special breed of sportsmen who year after year return to the wooded creek bottoms where the bird is found. Seldom easily visible in tangles of alders and willows, the woodcock has startled many an intruder by noisily launching itself straight up into an opening over the brush. In flight its wings make a sharp whistling noise; its mating song, also produced while the bird is in flight, can be heard around its favorite haunts on spring evenings. The frontispiece picture of a woodcock flying above alders was painted near Briggsville, Wisconsin, in 1953.

Philohela minor (Plate 30). Water color (16″ by 21″) owned by Dr. William Taylor, of Portage, Wisconsin.

Numbers refer to plates unless preceded by the word *page*.

Numbers refer to plates unless preceded by the word *page*.

LAKE SUPERIOR

APOSTLE
ISLANDS

Superior

BAYFIELD

DOUGLAS

ASHLAND

IRON

VILAS

WASHBURN

SAWYER

PRICE

ONEIDA

FOREST

FLORENCE

BURNETT

MARINETTE

POLK

BARRON

RUSK

LINCOLN

LANGLADE

OCONTO

WASHINGTON I.

TAYLOR

CLARK

MARATHON

Wausau

MENOMINEE

SHAWANO

GREEN BAY

DOOR

ST. CROIX

DUNN

CHIPPEWA

Chippewa R.

Eau Claire

PIERCE

PEPIN

EAU CLAIRE

BUFFALO

TREM-
PEALEAU

WOOD

PORTAGE

WAUPACA

OUTAGAMIE

KEWAU-
NEE

Green
Bay

JACKSON

Fox R.

BROWN

Appleton

JUNEAU

WAUSHARA

CAL-
UMET

MANITOWOC

MONROE

ADAMS

WINNEBAGO

Manitowoc

LA CROSSE

Fox R.

Oshkosh

Lake
Winnebago

La Crosse

MAR-
QUETTE

FOND DU
LAC

SHEBOY-
GAN

VERNON

GREEN
LAKE

Fond du
Lac

Sheboygan

SAUK

DODGE

WASH-
INGTON

OZAU-
KEE

LAKE
MICHIGAN

RICHLAND

CRAWFORD

Rock R.

0 10 20 30 40 50 Miles

COLUMBIA

Wisconsin R.

DANE

WAUKESHA

IOWA

Madison

JEFFERSON

Waukesha

MIL-
WAUKEE

Milwaukee

GRANT

Lake
Koshkonong

WALWORTH

RACINE

Racine

LAFAYETTE

GREEN

ROCK

Janesville

Kenosha

Beloit

KENOSHA

St. Croix R.

ST. CROIX

Mississippi

River

Black R.

Wisconsin R.